NOT HALF FREE

The Myth That America is Capitalist

By Walter Donway

With a preface by David Kelley

D1302067

Romantic Revolution Books

Not Half Free: The Myth that America is Capitalist

Not Half Free: The Myth that America is Capitalist

Copyright 2015 © Walter Donway

ISBN-13: 978-1511767873

Romantic Revolution Books
279 Stephen Hands Path
East Hampton, NY 11937
RomanticRevolutionBooks at Gmail.com

To my son, Ethan Donway,
For whose America I am fighting.

To my brother, Roger Donway,
With whom I have learned it all, lived it all.

Not Half Free: The Myth that America is Capitalist

Contents

Preface by David Kelley

Walter Donway and I have been friends since college days and comrades in the cause of liberty. For 20 years he served as a board member of The Atlas Society, an organization he helped me found to promote Ayn Rand's philosophy of Objectivism.

You may take that as full disclosure if you wish, but I mention it mainly to explain why I am proud to introduce and recommend this collection of Walter's articles on current issues.

Most of these articles have been published by the Atlas Society; the investment site, Financial Sense; or the new Objectivist-oriented Web site, *Savvy Street*. They represent Walter's observations and analysis of recent events. A third of them deal with the financial crisis in 2008-09 and the government response, the rest with other current issues.

Walter brings to these articles three assets that each stand out in their own right and in combination are unique. He is an astute and well-informed observer of contemporary issues. He is an accomplished novelist and poet who is a delight to read. And he is deeply grounded in philosophy, specifically the philosophy of Objectivism, bringing depth to his analysis of issues and exceptional clarity to his exposition.

The theme of *Not Half Free* is the decline of economic freedom. Those who value such freedom and have watched with dismay the growth of government control over the economy—especially under President Obama but beginning with G. W. Bush—will appreciate the acumen of Walter's analysis, issue by issue. But as he points out in his Introduction, such freedom and its decline are not salient to many Americans. Like frogs in slowly warming water, they accommodate to every new restriction. These are the people who most need this book. The core article in this regard is "U.S. Economic Freedom: Retreat Becomes Rout." If every voter in America read this piece, I think we would not be hurtling down the road to serfdom.

As an observer and commentator on the elements in the decline of economic freedom, Walter writes from his close observations of the economy and the effects of government intervention in financial markets, energy, health care, and many others. Though these essays are about recent events, he brings to bear his knowledge of the historical background. A primary example is "Health Care: The Road to Rationing," which shows how Obamacare's takeover of health care is a consequence of decisions made half a century ago. It's a depressing tale. As an antidepressant, read his articles about the good news in the fracking revolution in energy production and the decline of the OPEC cartel.

Not Half Free: The Myth that America is Capitalist

As a writer, Walter makes these issues come alive—even in talking about finance, inflation, and Federal Reserve policy. Economics has been called "the dismal science" in part because it is too often mind-numbing to read. Walter's articles are models of clarity and to-the-point analysis, even in his longer, more substantive pieces like "Nationalizing the Financial System." But his writer's skill is more clearly on display in the delightful pieces "How to Explain the Crash to Your Barber" and "A Buck for Your Thoughts" (a five-page lesson that tells you everything you need to know about inflation).

The latter essay is also a good example of Walter's philosophical depth. Philosophy has a reputation as an impossibly abstract and arcane discipline. As a philosopher, I'll admit there's some truth to that reputation. But I also have to say that philosophy is an immense asset in a writer. It can be a lens for seeing things more clearly, highlighting their essential features in abstraction from nonessential details. Writing about current events with his deep philosophical understanding, Walter is like a trained opera singer doing show-tunes, but with precision and power that show-tune singers can't match.

Walter is a lifelong student of philosophy and his philosophical depth is on display throughout *Not Half Free*. But I would recommend particularly "Bernie, Bernie, Was It 'Selfish'?" for addressing the core, controversial issue of self-interest in a market economy. If you read nothing else, please read this one. Discussing the case of Bernard Madoff whose Ponzi scheme caused investors millions of dollars in losses, Walter zeroes in with his philosophical lens on the central question and answers it with a narrative that is more effective than any abstract argument.

In the same vein, "Just Another Successful Business Man—Destroyed: The Ordeal of Greg Reyes," tells the story of a government and media assault on one of the Hank Reardens in our world; and "Sharia Zoning" makes the principle of property rights shine forth in a local municipal dispute.

Political acumen, a writer's skill, philosophical depth: You have a treat in store for you.

Introduction

"The U.S. is the only country to have recorded a loss of economic freedom each of the past seven years..." Since 2006, it "has suffered a dramatic decline of almost 6 points, with particularly large losses in property rights, freedom from corruption, and control of government spending. "...it is no longer one of the top 10 freest economies..."

(2014 Index of Economic Freedom)

Not everyone thinks in terms of "economic freedom." For some readers, the phrase denotes little or nothing. It seems to them in their job, their household budget, and their savings (if any) that there have been changes in the economy, perhaps disturbing changes, but not related to any sort of broad loss of "freedom." For others, "economic freedom" may bring to mind the complaints and demands of rich businessmen who protest against being regulated or taxed. For still others, it seems evident that America still is the world's greatest free economy—a triumph of market capitalism—and no changes have altered that.

What would those readers make of the headlines in a few financial publications in January 2014, reporting the 20ᵗʰ annual "Index of Economic Freedom"? For two decades, the *Index*, published by the Heritage Foundation and the *Wall Street Journal*, has systematically analyzed 186 countries on the basis of carefully chosen indices of economic freedom. As noted at the outset of this introduction, the *Index* in 2014 reported that economic freedom in the United States has declined for the seventh year in a row; no other nation in the world has experienced such a decline.

Of course, that in no way implies that the United States has become less economically free than most nations. Another rating of world economic freedom, entirely independent of the one cited above, is prepared in Canada by the prestigious Fraser Institute. Its reports have a two-year preparation period for gathering and analyzing statistics; thus, the 2014 report measured economic freedom up to the end of 2012. It had this to say about the United States:

"Throughout most of the period from 1980 to 2000, the United States ranked as the world's third freest economy, behind Hong Kong and Singapore…. [T]he United States in 2000 was [as rated on a scale of 1 to 10] 8.65, second only to Hong Kong. By 2005, the US rating had slipped to 8.20 and its ranking fallen to 9th. The slide has continued. The United States placed 15th in 2010 and 16th in 2011 before rebounding slightly to 14th in 2012."

That is to say, economic freedom in the United States remains greater than in most other nations. The point made by both reports is that the *decline in economic freedom* over more than a decade has been steady, steep, and relentless. But what does that *mean*?

Getting specific

This book, collecting essays written between 2009 and 2014—the very years of unbroken decline in American economic freedom—gets specific. The 18 essays, although on topics as diverse as America itself, and its economy, *all* tell stories of the decline of economic freedom. The virtue of these essays is not that they are complete or catalog the decline in freedom systematically and across the U.S. economy. Their virtue is that they build up the story, example by example, so that the phrase "economic freedom" becomes fleshed out, dressed, and walking.

It is not that the Heritage Foundation/*Wall Street Journal* and Fraser Institute reports are less than precise in their definitions of the categories of economic freedom—the indices that they are measuring. The Fraser Institute offers this overview of the causes of U.S. decline in economic freedom:

"What accounts for the US decline? While U.S. ratings and rankings have fallen in all five areas of the…index, the reductions have been largest in the Legal System and Protection of Property Rights (Area 2), Freedom to Trade Internationally (Area 4), and Regulation (Area 5). The plunge in Area 2 has been huge. In 2000, the 9.23 rating of the United States was the 9th highest in the world. But by 2012, the area rating had plummeted to 6.99, placing it 36th worldwide. While it is difficult to pinpoint the precise reason for the decline in Area 2, the increased use of eminent domain to transfer property to powerful political interests, the ramifications of the wars on terrorism and drugs, and the violation of the property rights of bondholders in the auto-bailout case have weakened the tradition of strong adherence to the rule of law in United States."

For a fuller look at the most recent Fraser report, how the reports are produced, and what data and interpretation they offer see the essay "U.S. Economic Freedom: Retreat Becomes Rout."

Nevertheless, these remain categories—some broader, some narrower. How, then, has the decline in economic freedom—in recent years a steady decline—played out day to day in corporations and small businesses, in Washington and city hall, on Wall Street and in the courts? What are the grim mechanics in America today of encroaching government control and the consequent shrinking of the domain of choosing, acting economic man? Exactly what are we losing that we care about—or should care about?

Those are the questions answered in these 18 essays, which range from a report on how we are "nationalizing the financial system" to a snapshot of how one Long Island town exercises plenipotentiary power over property rights in the name of zoning. To alert the reader to how these diverse pieces may give life to the "Index of Economic Freedom," it is worth listing the "10 freedoms" on which the *Index* annually rates a nation in order to reach a composite score for economic freedom as a whole. Then, we may ask how the essays in this book give specificity, even drama and passion, and poignancy, to these categories.

Can we talk about 'economic' freedom?

Before undertaking that, let us look briefly at one other implication of this book's title: *Not Half Free*. Is it justified? Is the U.S. economy, today, really less than half free? No toting up of categories or ratings will add up to that conclusion. But it remains crucial to ask how far we have travelled the road to what Frederick Hayek called "serfdom."

We first must specify that the question applies to *economic freedom*. The need to make that distinction, however, introduces a potentially dangerous confusion because the attempt to separate so-called "economic rights" from human rights, or "economic freedom" from human freedom, is one of the greatest threats to freedom itself. Human freedom is unitary, indivisible, and incapable of surviving any attempted partitioning. The reason is as fundamental as the unity of mind and body that constitutes the human being. The mind thinks and chooses, the body acts. The mind dreams, conceives, and invents; the body pursues, creates, and consumes.

The philosopher who articulated this best and has armed us to defend human rights without fatal contradictions was Ayn Rand. In her essay, "Man's Rights," in *The Virtue of Selfishness*, she wrote:

"The right to life is the source of all rights—and the right to property is their only implementation. Without property rights, no other rights are possible. Since man has to sustain his life by his own effort, the man who has no right to the product of his effort has no means to sustain his life. The man who produces, while others dispose of his product, is a slave."

The *U.S. Constitution*—and the men who wrote it and those who ratified it—certainly intended property to have the same protection as the rights to speech, press, assembly, religion, due process, and all our other liberties. State constitutions drafted during the same period explicitly named "property" as among man's inalienable rights. And so it was understood in the Nineteenth Century, with protection of property actually increasing throughout much of the century.

It was the impact of the Marxist view of man's destiny, the notion that the sole deciding factor in the affairs of men are economic forces—and that ideas are mere rationalizations for existing economic relations—that cleaved the view of man's rights. Arriving in America from German universities in the later decades of the Nineteenth Century, Marxism split "economic rights" off from religious rights, intellectual rights, and civil rights—from liberty itself.

In fact, they are all human rights, the "rights of man," and as inseparable in reality, in our lives, as our minds and bodies. But, today, "liberty," all the rights enumerated in the Bill of Rights of *U.S. Constitution*, is defended by "liberals," "progressives," and conservatives alike. The Supreme Court can be relied upon to rule in their favor and the media rally to their defense. Any violation of those rights is viewed as a dangerous precedent to be rejected out of hand; they are a matter of principle—as they should be.

Economic rights enjoy no such reverence, no reliable affirmation in our courts, no spirited editorial defense in the news media. And that, in very briefest terms, is why in recent years we could read such headlines as "America's Dwindling Economic Freedom" (*Wall Street Journal*, January 13, 2014) and "US Plunges in Economic Freedom Index" (*Chief Executive*, January 10, 2013)—and register little national interest, much less alarm.

For many Americans, as mentioned at the outset of this introduction, the reality was that "economic freedom" either meant nothing at all—evoked no specifics, no referents in their lives—or, along Marxist lines, stood for a mere partisan strategy of the economically powerful—or failed to dent a settled confidence in the American economy.

And so we must be cautious, must add many qualifications, when we set out to measure "economic freedom"—and both of the reporting systems, in their own way, do this. In this context, we may ask how much of our economic freedom we have lost—knowing that the answer unavoidably refers to freedom itself.

"Half free"?

Actually, one can state a single figure that roughly captures the *direct* tax burden on productive Americans, on our economic output as a whole. The Tax Policy Institute supplies such a figure each year. For 2008, taxes of all kinds in the United States, on all levels, amounted to 28 percent of the country's total production (Gross Domestic Product). Government is taxing away and spending between one-quarter and one-third of everything we produce. This is still less than one dollar out of every three, if you find that reassuring. But the figure is a misleading proxy for the extent of government's domination of our efforts and resources—and so our choices and plans.

For one thing, perhaps the most obvious, Washington is spending far more than it collects in taxes. Hugely increasing our national debt by selling U.S. Treasury bonds, government is mortgaging our economic output far into the future, tying up taxes that we and our children will pay for decades to come. That process and the political forces that drive it are discussed in many essays in this volume.

Having piled up debt to levels at which other countries are rebelling at further lending to us, Washington is simply creating the money needed for more spending. But every time government creates a new dollar that dollar lessens the value of all dollars already in existence. More dollars chasing the same amount of goods drives all prices higher—or, which is the same thing, reduces what any dollar can buy, debases our money.

And that is only the most obvious way, beyond direct taxation, that government commandeers our production and earnings. A still more destructive burden on production is the suffocating coil of government regulation, relentlessly enwrapping us and tightening. The burden of regulation on the freedom to produce must be measured not only in hundreds of billions of dollars spent to comply with virtually incomprehensible numbers of regulations—the time and expense of lawyers and accountants, executives and staffs—but the lost value of production that is forbidden, made too costly, or made too legally risky.

In brief, these are estimated costs to the U.S. economy of regulation (from Tax Reform's "Center for

Fiscal Accountability"). Each year, compliance with government regulations (in terms of time, professional services, and equipment) consumes about 17.7 percent of U.S. national income. The cost of compliance does not include the economic impact of regulations in limiting production or distorting economic choices. The best available estimate of *that* regulatory damage to the economy is $1 trillion a year. Apart from both those burdens is the cost to government (that is, taxpayers) of enforcing the regulations: about $61 billion a year.

Add up the burden of taxation by government at all levels; wealth drained away by debt and money creation; and the burden of regulation. It is more than plausible that we are "not half free" in our economic lives—and last I heard only ghosts lead lives unaffected by the economy. But, above all, the message of this introduction, and book of essays, is that rapidly, relentlessly, we have been getting *less free*.

"10 freedoms" and what it means to lose them

Finally, look briefly at the "10 freedoms" rated each year by the Heritage Foundation/*Wall Street Journal* index and how the essays you are about to read make specific, often poignant, what we have lost—and even now are losing.

Property rights. The principle of the right to property, fully and consistently recognized and protected, can be equated with economic freedom itself. If all citizens are free, without exception, to produce and dispose of what they produce, they are free and so is their country. The essay "Crony Capitalism versus Making Money" views the days and weeks of the 2008 financial crisis as the climax of "cronyism," by which wealth is obtained—not earned or created—by political connections, by political "pull." In the frantic, secret negotiations between Washington power brokers and frightened, intimidated businessmen, the dissolution or survival, the subsidizing or jettisoning, of major banks, Wall Street brokerages, and other businesses was decided by horse-trading and political clout. Property rights were trampled in the dust.

On a wholly different scale, but just as surely, the meeting of the local zoning board in the town of East Hampton (see "Sharia Zoning") dictates to businesses and property owners what they may and may not do with their property. The deciding principle is not property rights but criteria such as "the character of the town" and the aesthetics of the landscape.

Freedom from corruption. Cronyism is the very definition of corruption: the direction and disposal of economic affairs not by the choices, agreements, and rights of owners, but by means of deals with those in power at every level of government. The dissection of cronyism is continued in the essay "Nationalizing the Financial System," the story of the months and then years after the financial crisis and stock-market crash during which government locked its grip on America's financial industry—in the name of "reforms" that should have been directed at government and the crony regime, not at private businesses.

Fiscal freedom. We have touched on government taxation and spending, the most direct way government takes wealth from those who earn it and own it to spend on some conception of the "public good" or "national interest." The financial crisis and ensuing stock-market crash and "Great Recession" provided Washington with excuses for spending that more than doubled the national debt—the totality of debt accumulated since the U.S. Government began—in less than a decade.

"The Theme Song is 'Yuan the Magic Dragon'" zeroes in on one outcome of that spending spree. Governments such as that of the People's Republic of

China, who have loaned trillions of dollars to the United States, and now see U.S. debt becoming unsustainable—and the value of the dollar itself in long-term decline—are taking the first steps toward replacing the U.S. dollar as the unit of international exchange and trade. Will the "mighty U.S. dollar" be supplanted by the "mighty Chinese Yuan"? That is the long-term strategy of the ancient Dragon Throne—and they are patient.

Government spending. What government spends, of course, is the other face of taxation, debt, and money creation. Today, spending at a level unknown in our history is driven by cronyism, the influence of lobbyists for hundreds of special interests, all fighting to direct more spending to themselves. This theme runs through virtually every essay in this book because today the American government dispenses riches unknown in the history of the world. But here we encounter an iron logic: With government money comes government control, as described in "Health Care—The Road to Rationing," an overview of how the great American medical care system has become government's biggest spending program—and a budget time-bomb as demands of an aging population soar—and also one of the most heavily controlled and regulated sector of our economy.

Business freedom. The story of the years after the financial panic of 2008 has been accelerated regulation of the U.S. financial industry that amounted to nationalization. This is not the "socializing" of an industry that occurs under garden-variety socialism; it is thoroughgoing government control of businesses that remain, only in name, private. But if ownership means "the right to use and dispose" of property, then the nationalizing of America's single largest industry is well advanced. A poignant personal story of catastrophic loss of freedom is told in "Just another Successful Business Man—Destroyed: The Ordeal of Greg Reyes."

Labor freedom. Labor legislation and regulations—including union freedom to negotiate, but also freedom of workers from government-backed union coercion—make labor an isolatable sphere of economic freedom. In most of this book's essays, "laborers" are treated as what they are: producers. What affects all producers affects them. Regulations affect not only our work, but prices we pay, and products that become available (or never do). As Federal budgets metastasize and solemn vows to cut spending keep failing—all cuts are too painful to *someone*—there is another aspect of regulation to consider: it hugely hampers the productivity of our economy. Just can't cut spending? How about, as a first step, enabling us to produce more? The case is made in "A New Way to Fix the Debt Crisis: Unchain Atlas."

Monetary freedom. Few areas of freedom have been so systematically invaded and ravaged over the past decade as savings, interest rates, and exchange values in trade. All are critically affected by the soundness of money: its freedom from arbitrary manipulation by government, including above all the U.S. Federal Reserve system ("Fed"). Money is our medium for exchanging goods, saving our wealth, and managing our economic future. If we cannot rely on its value—if its value is subject to constant manipulation by bureaucrats—then what does the right to property mean? For more than a century, the Federal Reserve system has been the manipulator-in-chief of the U.S. dollar, as described in "A Buck for Your Thoughts," fueling a cycle of economic boom and bust, eroding the value of the dollar to just pennies, and bleeding the value from everyone's savings in every decade.

Trade freedom. Since the early 1970s, U.S. foreign trade—including the balance of imports over exports—has been skewed, sometimes wildly, by the international cartel called the Organization of Petroleum Exporting Countries (OPEC). Decades of rhetoric about

U.S. "energy independence" have remained just that—talk. Government deserves much of the blame for having crushed domestic oil, gas, and coal production under a steamroller of regulations and limitations inspired by environmentalists.

But by 2014, what must be called the "semi-free" market seemed to have prevailed over the cartel, with North American oil and natural gas producers employing new technology, including "fracking," to become world leaders in petroleum production. By mid-year, the pricing power of the cartel appeared to be crumbling, and, by year's end, the international price of oil was in "free fall." The story is told, here, in two essays: "U.S. and Canadian Oil Drillers Frack the OPEC Cartel" and "Competition Finally Upsets the Biggest Monopoly of All: OPEC."

As world oil prices plunged from more than $110 a barrel to $55 a barrel in just four months, those who understand what makes markets work laughed at the utter silence from Washington about the role of "speculators" in the precipitous price action. Less than two years earlier, President Obama had given a threatening lecture on how "speculators" had driven up the price of oil—and must be blamed for sky-high prices at the gas pump. The story is told in the essay "Obama's Power Move: Scapegoating Speculators."

Investment freedom. Both "investment freedom" and "financial freedom" (the tenth and final category in the freedom *Index*, discussed below) have been transformed since 2007–8, with all change in the direction of loss of economic freedom. Laws enacted in the wake of the financial crisis, including the "Dodd-Frank" legislation, imposed a level of supervision and regulation on the financial industry that many saw as insupportable. As yet, the full weight of that massive regulatory straitjacket has not been felt; but its extent, costs, and ultimate futility are exposed in "Nationalizing the Financial System." The most egregious financial fraud of our time, which arrested the nation's attention on the trial of Bernard Madoff and his life sentence, suggests not a lack of regulation but the futility of such regulation. "Bernie, Bernie, Was It 'Selfish'?" tells the story.

Financial freedom. In the years covered by essays in this book, financial freedom suffered grievous losses. That could have been predicted by the middle of 2008, when the financial crisis and stock-market plunge peaked. Government's pattern has been to use every crisis to seize additional power. Those who approve that process say that crisis is the opportunity to impose needed reform; but the "reform" rarely is of government—and never by reducing government's power. And yet, as these essays demonstrate, again and again, the cause of every *systemic* economic crisis is government intervention. Quite simply: No company or industry is large enough, has enough capacity to accumulate debt, and can get so financially over-extended as to threaten a nation's—or the world's—economy, as the financial crisis of 2008 did.

But how to expose the big lie that more government makes us safer from periodic crises—crises that mysteriously keep getting worse as government accretes more power? The essay "How to Explain the Crash to Your Barber" offers an alternate narrative of the origin, causes, and culprits of the financial crisis and the economic hardship that followed.

By the end of this book, the reader will have hundreds of examples of what the author views as "economic freedom," and ways that governments diminish freedom. Each reader will judge not only if economic freedom truly was at stake, but, if so, was its limitation justified by some higher value.

The author's fondest hope, though—a kind of baseline goal—is that no reader finishes this book not knowing what "economic freedom" is—or not caring.

Walter Donway
East Hampton, NY
January 2015

Crony Capitalism versus "Making" Money (May 2012)

Saluting the philosopher who gave reason its foundational tool, Ayn Rand named the three sections of her epic novel, *Atlas Shrugged*, after Aristotle's axioms of logic. The second section, "Either-Or," is the novel's pivot. The heroes of the novel face a choice: either cooperate with an advancing dictatorship—by struggling to keep producing despite the tightening stranglehold of regulations—or refuse to work, to produce, in the absence of freedom.

To do the latter means to witness the proliferation of a breed of businessman eager to curry favor with politicians whose power can enable a business to defeat rivals without the need to do a better job. Today, the system that spawns and rewards that breed of businessman has a name: "crony capitalism."

How people interpret that phrase reveals what is at stake. To the great economists of free trade and free markets, from Adam Smith and David Ricardo to Ludwig von Mises and Milton Friedman, capitalism meant *laissez faire* ("let us compete free of government help or hindrance"). To them, *laissez faire* in the phrase "*laissez faire* capitalism" was redundant. To opponents of capitalism, today, such as leftist MIT Professor Noam Chomsky or sociologist Jane Jacobs, "crony capitalism" is the redundant phrase. They believe that capitalism by its nature involves corruption of the political process to favor one enterprise over another.

What about the American public? On January 18, 2012, a poll by the Rasmussen firm revealed that 39 percent of those responding consider ours a system of "crony capitalism." And they are right. But that does not answer the question: Does it *have* to be?

Defining "crony capitalism"

What is "crony capitalism"? The *Wikipedia* definition will serve: "an economy in which success in business depends on close relationships between business and government officials. It may be exhibited by favoritism in the distribution of legal permits, government grants, special tax breaks, and so forth."

The reign of cronyism throws into relief two radically different breeds of businessman: the one who profits by innovating, producing, cost-cutting, and winning customers—and the one who prospers by means of "pull" in Washington, the state capital, or town hall.

In *Atlas Shrugged*, Orren Boyle is able to "tame" the competition of Hank Rearden and his revolutionary invention, Rearden Metal, only by using political pull to win regulations and quotas that cripple Rearden. The consummate crony capitalist, James Taggart, "helps" his company's struggling railroad line in Colorado by getting his pals in Washington to create an "anti-dog-eat-dog" rule that shackles its enterprising rival, the Phoenix-Durango line. Any reader who cares about ability or merit is outraged, then disgusted, as the innovators and entrepreneurs in *Atlas Shrugged* are betrayed, then crippled, by the manipulations of businessmen who thrive on pull with their cronies in Washington.

"Crony Capitalism" on the campaign trail

Crony capitalism has been around for a long time. It plagued the great era of railroad building in nineteenth-century America, when huge subsidies and land grants were given for proposed lines—some never built. But the event that put the term itself into the active vocabulary of the American public, I believe, was the massive government intervention in private business that followed the financial panic of 2008. If, today, almost 40 percent of Americans identify our system as "crony capitalism," we may hope that they also know—or are open to learning about—real capitalism.

As the 2012 Presidential election heats up, we are likely to hear the term with increasing frequency. Mitt Romney, now front-runner for the Republican nomination for president, published an op-ed article in the *Detroit News* on February 14 accusing President Barack Obama of "crony capitalism on a grand scale."

He said, in part, "A labor union that had contributed millions to Democrats and his election campaign was granted an ownership share of Chrysler and a major stake in GM, two flagships of the industry. The US Department of Treasury—American taxpayers—was asked to become a majority stockholder of GM. And a politically connected and ethically challenged Obama-campaign contributor, the financier Steven Rattner, was asked to preside over all this as auto czar."

I quote Mr. Romney not as endorsement, but to provide an example of how "crony capitalism" has entered the vocabulary of the 2012 Presidential election. If you Google "crony capitalism," you will find references to "crony capitalism" in dozens of publications both for and against Barack Obama.

Must capitalism be cronyism?

Capitalism is distinguished from every other economic system (such as socialism, fascism, feudalism, or syndicalism) by the degree of involvement of government in the economy. Capitalism is the economic system that emerges when government recognizes the right to private property, private enterprise, free competition, and private profit—the right, not permission or sufferance when those in power deem an activity "in the public interest." The term *"laissez faire"* is added for emphasis to make clear that when government intervenes to limit property rights, freedom of enterprise, and trade, the system no longer is capitalism. There is a well-recognized term for the new system: "mixed economy"—a mixture of freedom and controls. It is not "capitalism" when every business can thrive—or die—depending upon political influence.

Those who insist that the rich and powerful always will exert their influence to extract favors and advantage from politicians and bureaucrats may welcome this advice: Devise a government strictly limited by its constitution (as did America's Founding Fathers) so that politicians and bureaucrats simply don't have the power to help or hinder business. Then there will be no use lobbying, bribing, or putting friends into office. Do not say that capitalism is impossible without cronyism until you separate government and the economy in the same absolute way that the *U.S. Constitution* separates government and religion.

We see, today, the result of decades and decades of relentless efforts to erode the separation of government and economy. Businessmen themselves often spearheaded these efforts; they were the type of businessman who finds it easier to get a subsidy than earn a profit, easier to shackle a rival than compete. Other businessmen fought the encroachment of regulation, the taxation of some for the benefit of others, and the erection of trade barriers to "help" home industries.

Crony capitalism in action

Cronyism differs from industry to industry. That variation depends on the extent to which a field is regulated, on how much those regulations are subject to interpretation, and, especially, on whether government is a major payer (as in medical and hospital care) or can give or withhold the permission literally to exist (as in mining or energy production). Today, a Wall Street firm will contribute millions to the election of both Democrats and Republicans because it dares not risk lacking "access" to the White House and Congress. The firm's "investment" has nothing to do with innovation, production, or meeting demands of customers. It may be buying protection against political power in exactly the way a restaurant owner in Brooklyn must buy "protection" when the mob comes seeking a cut of his profits. Or it may be buying the political influence to shape regulations and taxes in ways that give it an advantage over competitors.

There also are corporations virtually built on government influence, for whose executives lobbying is a "core competency." In 2008, Fannie Mae and Freddie Mac, the biggest mortgage-financing firms in America, were publicly-owned, profit-making companies, listed on the New York Stock Exchange. They also were creations of government (designated "government sponsored enterprises"). In the run-up to the 2008 financial panic, they spent huge sums lobbying Congress to win permission to leverage their mortgage investments far beyond limits set on any private bank. They purchased and "securitized" huge numbers of mortgages from banks—enabling those banks to lend still more. Investigations into the complex causes of the real-estate bubble and the deceptive packaging of sub-prime mortgages—and thus the financial panic and recession that followed—routinely point to the role of "Fannie" and "Freddie."

As the gargantuan "Patient Protection and Affordable Care Act" (known as "Obama care") was debated in Congress, hundreds of hospitals, physician groups, pharmaceutical corporations, and medical technology companies besieged Congress to fight for the inclusion or exclusion of sections of the Act that could affect their profits or their very survival. The orgy of horse trading continued until the day the Act passed. It was as though armies were locked in battle to fight and die for every inch of ground.

Professional organizations and associations, businesses, and their lobbyists spent millions, as earlier they had spent millions in campaign contributions to the Congressman—or President—on whom they now called for favors.

But can one succeed without a "crony"?

There is a clear and honest choice between achievement and manipulation—in principle. But today we must take care in applying that distinction. The bureaucrat's power to help or hinder, enable profit or inflict loss, is so pervasive—at times, decisive—that no businessman can ignore it.

Fairness obliges us to make distinctions, and we have a touchstone. It comes from the pivotal second section of *Atlas Shrugged*, where Francisco d'Anconia makes one of the most rousing expositions of an idea ever penned for a fictional character. The setting is the wedding of James Taggart, one of the pull-peddlers-in-chief, an occasion swarming with men grown rich as politicians and their cronies feast on the last of the country's wealth. Someone throws out the hackneyed phrase "money is the root of all evil…" and Francisco replies with a defense of money that pierces to the roots of human morality.

At the climax of the speech, he says: "If you ask me to name the proudest distinction of Americans, I would choose—because it contains all the others—the fact that they were the people who created the phrase 'to make money.' …Americans were the first to understand that wealth has to be created."

Is a businessman, today, who is struggling to navigate through the shoals of regulations and permissions, nevertheless engaged in the creation of new goods or services, the "making" of money? Or are his negotiations with politicians and bureaucrats the activity that in itself gets the money—through subsidies, stifling of competition, or new regulations that channel profits into his business?

Consider just one example: The world today is hungry for copper to build the infrastructure of new industrial civilizations in China and India. But to open a new copper mine in the United States or Canada, say, you need permission from environmental agencies on the federal, state (or provincial), and local levels. Obtaining these permissions can require years of costly studies to satisfy hundreds of regulatory conditions. The judges are bureaucrats at all levels, usually under pressure from dozens of conflicting lobbies. Hundreds of millions of dollars ride on their decision. They may be ideologically opposed to "exploiting" natural resources (as are many in the Obama administration). To surmount their dogged opposition, you may need a politician who applauds your goal and can run interference for you. The goal is to clear the path to the production of copper—and making money.

Why they came to Washington

The businessmen, doctors, and hospital administrators who flocked to Washington to try to influence the Obamacare behemoth—and spent millions on well-connected professional lobbyists (almost half of former Congressmen in the private sector are registered lobbyists)—did so for one reason. In our crony capitalist system, government has the power to advance or set back the profits, career, and income of anyone who works for a living.

That power, growing decade after decade in America, makes cronyism inevitable. As government intervention and spending have burgeoned, so has the constant stream of petitioners to Washington or state capitals, seeking what they need or want from politicians and bureaucrats. In 2009, the U.S. Chamber of Commerce, the country's largest lobbying group, spent $144.5 million on lobbying; it has 150 lobbyists working on its behalf. ExxonMobil spent $27.4 million. The American Association of Retired People (AARP) spent $21 million. The American Association of Realtors spent $19.5 million. The American Beverage Association spent $18.8 million. In total, since 1998, just the top 20 lobbying groups spent more than $4.0 billion. But these sums, which count only direct lobbying expenses, are dwarfed by the total expenditures—and the millions of hours—organizations divert to influencing government.

The solution is the one that shapes the philosophy of the *U.S. Constitution*: strictly and sharply define and delimit the powers that government is given. Put government back in the business of protecting property rights and upholding a basic framework of laws: the kind of laws enforced by the police and courts—not by regulators and dispensers of trillions of dollars for plans and goals imposed or approved by government.

Do not think that those regulations and trillions of dollars of largesse are dispensed in "the public interest"? Government cannot discern, cannot fathom, the "public" interest amidst the countless daily choices, plans, and actions of hundreds of millions of individuals and businesses anticipating the future. In reality, the regulations and largesse are spoils won in the ceaseless war of pressure group against pressure group to seize the transitory advantage of political favor. They can be nothing else.

When Crony Capitalism Went Mad

As I mentioned earlier, there was one development more than any other that put "crony capitalism" into the vocabulary of the American people and thrust it into the 2012 election campaign.

In September 2008, as the financial panic began to unfold, Treasury Secretary Henry Paulson—who came to the Bush administration from the chairmanship of Goldman Sachs, Wall Street's most powerful and successful investment bank and securities firm—engaged in a frantic round of closed-door meetings with banks, brokerage houses, and insurance companies. It seemed as though at the close of every weekend a new bombshell dropped: the venerable Lehman Brothers would be "permitted" to fail; the legendary Merrill-Lynch would be forced into a shotgun marriage with Bank of America, American International Group (a multinational insurance company) would be saved…and so it went. Government officials and executives of financial firms, we were reminded, were making decisions to "save the financial system," to prevent another "Great Depression."

To pay for it all, legislation proposed by Secretary Paulson was rammed through Congress in the atmosphere of rising panic. It included the Troubled Assets Relief Program (TARP) that provided an initial $700 billion in taxpayer funds to Wall Street brokers, investment banks, and insurance companies. The "troubled assets" of those firms were private assets, which they willingly had bought. This was only the beginning. There followed a complete opening of the U.S. Treasury, and the Federal Reserve with its statutory authority to create new money without limit, to "rescue" Fannie Mae and Freddie Mac, bail out General Motors and Chrysler, and purchase trillions of dollars in "toxic securities" from banks. Americans discovered that their national debt had increased by trillions of dollars.

Washington declared that the U.S. and, indeed, the international financial system had been saved from catastrophe. But from October 3, when TARP was enacted, to March 6, 2009, the flagship U.S. stock-market index, the S&P 500, plunged from 1200 to 666. Stock markets all over the world crashed and the American economy was heading into a slump so severe that it was labeled "the Great Recession." Millions of Americans lost their retirement accounts in the stock market crash; for the first time in memory housing prices plunged year after year and mortgage defaults soared; and unemployment rose toward 10 percent (according to official government sources, although private tallies place it at 16 percent).

In government offices, university economics departments, and the news media the almost unanimous opinion, today, remains that government and financial executives—reaching deals in the frantic nights and weekends of autumn, 2008—saved us from catastrophe. Considerably fewer than half of Americans polled in 2010 accept this justification for TARP and all that followed.

My point, here, is not to judge the specific, short-term outcomes of this truly unprecedented intervention in the American economy. Its effects, including trillions in new national debt and historic money creation (inflation) by the Federal Reserve, are still unfolding—and will for years to come. My point is that government and "private" business became indistinguishable in determining "who got what," who had to be "saved" and who did not—and that this is not capitalism.

Apparently, a large plurality of Americans know this and are sick of it. They do not call it "capitalism" because it is not capitalism—and because they respect the historic benefits of wealth and liberty, unprecedented in human history, that capitalism delivers.

No, they call it "crony capitalism."

Published in *Financial Sense Online*, May, 7, 2012.

Nationalizing the Financial Industry
(May, 2012)

When government proposes to nationalize a major industry, it is a loudspeaker blaring the message that the country is abandoning the market economy, moving from capitalism to socialism. So it has been in Venezuela as socialist President Hugo Chavez nationalized oil-drilling, gold-mining, coffee producing, and other industries. When nationalizations begin, capital flees a country, businessmen despair, and socialists cheer the death of private property.

But no one is talking about nationalizing American business, right? There are no decrees transferring businesses from private ownership to government "ownership." And no panicked flight of capital or despairing businessmen.

And yet, the largest sector of American enterprise, the sector at the heart of capitalism, because it is at the heart of investment—the valuation of companies, and the exchange businesses, commodities, and money worldwide—is being nationalized rapidly, massively, and perhaps irreversibly. The financial sector, Wall Street—the worldwide historic icon of capitalism—is far along the road to government control and de facto government ownership.

Adding up the trends

In a sense, the steps have been obvious, but an article in the *Economist* "put it all together" for me. It appeared on May 26, in the famous "Buttonwood" column (named for the tree under which the first, rudimentary 'stock market' began in New York City, seen as the precursor of Wall Street). Its title was "The Nationalisation of Markets: The Rise of the Financial-Political Complex."

The article identified trends reported daily, but made the point that the scale of those trends, the extent to which they shape the financial industry, and the dependence of the financial industry on them amounts to the "creeping nationalization" of the industry. The steps by which this is occurring are complex in their interactions, and nearly untraceable in their full effects—but nevertheless sweeping in scope.

Please consider this essay not an analysis of this complex process, but an alert, a warning to heed what is befalling the financial sector--and to oppose it.

Growth, dominance, takeover

The financial industry is the single largest sector in the U.S. economy as measured by the weighting of financial stocks within the flagship S&P 500 Index of the country's premier public companies. For many years, up to 2008, the financial sector kept growing until it reached 21 percent of the S&P 500 index. With the financial panic of 2008 and the crash of 2008-2009, the capital of financial companies plunged and so did their weighting in the index. Briefly, technology became the largest sector; but, by 2010, finance was moving again into first place.

None of this timing is accidental—either in terms of the growing dominance of the financial sector or its accelerating takeover by government. As many industries (such as health care) have discovered, the earliest government involvement often super-charges growth and profits, as government funds pour in and government acts to privilege the industry in the market. Later comes the government control, always with the argument that, since government has a huge stake in the industry, it must regulate it. Soon, the inevitable economic distortions caused by government intervention (such as soaring prices of medical care services as a result of offering them free of charge to millions of people and adding the expense of many layers of government bureaucracy) breed crises—and government steps in with more controls as savior.

This pattern has occurred in the financial industry. Starting in the late 1980s, the United States entered a generation-long credit expansion fueled by Federal Reserve Board ("Fed") policies of keeping interest rates historically low and inflating the money supply. In 2000, after the bursting of the stock market technology bubble (especially the frenzied investment in new ".com" enterprises), the Fed came to the rescue of the market with historically low interest rates. Over the next decade, the Fed watched its policies inflate a vast credit bubble in the real-estate industry; but the credit expansion also affected the balance sheets (savings, borrowing, and debt) of consumers, businesses, and state and local governments. In 2008, that credit bubble burst, precipitating the first full-scale financial panic since 1907, a sickening plunge in the stock markets, and, subsequently, the deepest recession since the Great Depression of the 1930s.

Again, the process was immensely complicated—and that is part of the reason government's accelerating involvement, and now the virtual nationalization, of the financial industry is so difficult to oppose. For example, in the bitter aftermath of the 2008-2009 panic and stock market crash, as the country slid into recession, many blamed the disaster on the greed, mismanagement, and irresponsibility of bankers, real-estate companies, mortgage brokers, and investment bankers.

But "greed," the desire for profits, is ever-present in the economy and motivates its growth, the success of individuals and companies, and the creation of wealth. And mismanagement, irresponsibility, bad practices, and fly-by-night companies are always present, too. The question is: how did these problems become so widespread, influential, and ultimately almost ubiquitous in the real-estate field (and in banks, brokerages, insurance companies, and others with investments tied to that field)? The answer, in large part, is that the huge credit expansion driven by the Fed—and exacerbated in real estate, in particular, by two government-created agencies with the now-infamous names "Fannie Mae" and "Freddie Mac"—pushed the industry into over-drive, and, at the same time, disabled all the usual restraints such as rising interest rates, increasing risk-aversion, and lack of additional capital for investment.

In summer 2008, as the huge real-estate bubble, and all the financial instruments based on it—many packaging or "securitizing" increasingly shoddy mortgages—began to burst, sheer panic seized the markets. The unfolding of these events is well known, now.

This was the pivotal moment when, having intervened for years in ways that distorted the real-estate industry, and involved the credit and home values of consumers as well as the investments of banks, brokers, and insurance companies worldwide, the government stepped in to save the financial industry (and, it is claimed, the entire international financial system) by arrogating to itself enormous new powers. The nationalizing of the financial sector began in earnest.

In the dark days of the panic in fall 2008, the U.S. Treasury, the Fed, and other government agencies held virtually non-stop meetings with executives of America's largest banks, investment companies, brokerages, and insurance companies at which they decided the fate of firms such as Bear-Sterns, Lehman Brothers, Bank of America, Merrill Lynch, American International Group (AIG), Washington Mutual, and dozens more. At the same time, the Treasury and Fed made truly unprecedented investments of taxpayer money in financial firms—a "rescue" for which many (but not all) financial executives pleaded. Reluctant to act, at first, Congress became panicked—as the markets plunged seemingly endlessly—into approving hundreds of billions of dollars for the financial bailout.

Creeping, then galloping, nationalization

That was the dramatic phase of the nationalization, the fireworks of the takeover. In a sense, it was presented as being reversible, with companies obligated to pay back the huge government infusions of cash to regain their independence. The more thorough, systematic government assumption of effective control of the financial industry unfolded during the long recession that has followed the panic and crash. I will cite only a few broad examples:

First, in its historic role as "recession" fighter, the Fed periodically had lowered short-term interest rates (the only rates it directly controls) to expand credit, spur bank loans, and relieve debt-stressed companies and consumers. These typically were temporary measures, with the Fed then moving to raise rates as the economy improved. But as the current deep recession has dragged on, the Fed has announced that it would keep short-term interest rates effectively at zero for years—until 2015 was the latest decision. And it has moved to use its powers to influence long-term rates, as well.

Interest rates affect the cost of borrowing and what interest bank depositors can get on their deposits; they help to determine banks' profits; they are the motor of the huge debt market (government and corporate bonds, for example); they directly affect the valuation of stocks (which compete with bonds as investments); and have other fundamental functions in the economy. Interest rates are the engine that drives the financial sector, and, through it, the entire economy. Today, increasingly, it is not the market that steers this engine, but government.

Second, government, always big in the bond markets, has become dominant. In order to borrow, government sells its short-term and long-term debt—now trillions of dollars, much of it owed to the People's Republic of China, Japan, and the Arab states. During the recession, though, the Treasury and Fed became purchasers of private debt, spending hundreds of billions of dollars buying "distressed" mortgage-backed securities and other types of debt with which banks, brokerages, and insurance companies were stuck. As a result, American taxpayers became the owners of this otherwise unmarketable debt.

In addition, though, as the "Buttonwood" column points out, as the Fed flooded the banking system with money, including by means of pure money creation (inflation), the banks responded by purchasing government bonds. That's right; instead of making loans that were supposed to "get the economy moving," the terrified banks—not knowing who could or could not repay loans in the still chaotic financial system—used the Fed's money to buy government debt. Hence the subtitle used by Buttonwood, "The Rise of the Financial-Political Complex."

Third, the Fed has made the entire U.S. stock market (and, as a side effect, stock markets worldwide) dependent on its policies. In the depths of the stock market crash in mid-2009, the Fed announced aggressive interest-rate cuts and other policies to inject money into the economy. The stock markets rallied, or, more descriptively, rocketed higher. As the Fed's "easing" policies came to an end, however, the markets sagged and then began to plunge.

Accommodatingly, the Fed announced the next round of cash injection, this time including outright money creation—inflation—euphemistically called "quantitative easing." The markets again rocketed. For the first time, a Fed chairman, Ben Bernanke, actually stated—in an Op-Ed article in the *Washington Post*—that an explicit goal of the Fed was to boost the stock market and so create profits that would be spent and stimulate businesses.

The response of the economy itself to this huge "stimulus" (the financial field is full of euphemistic terms for government intervention) has been unclear—but never very strong and with scant effect on, say, unemployment. But any chart setting side by side the timing of the Fed's easing and the rise and fall of the stock market indices makes abundantly clear that the markets of the world's largest, most important financial system now respond like Pavlov's dogs to the actions of the Fed.

As of this writing, the Fed has sought to yank the markets out of yet another decline in spring, 2012, by a rather weak third round of "easing." This time, the response of the markets has been disappointment, but expectations are that, as the economy continues to weaken, and the November Presidential election nears, the Fed will launch full-scale "quantitative easing" (inflation).

Lastly, as government money and activity became dominant in interest rates, debt, and the financial markets— three keys to the economy—the government also created and enacted, on largely party (Democratic) lines, legislation that gave Congress and the executive branch virtually unlimited power to regulate and reorganize the entire U.S. financial system. The Dodd-Frank bill was passed by a Democratic Congress and on July 21, 2010, President Obama signed it into law. The 869-page "Wall Street Reform and Consumer Protection Act," which the *Wall*

Street Journal reported will require 387 *sets* of rules to implement, creates an omnibus federal oversight committee charged with identifying "potential threats to U.S. financial stability" and with "regulatory proposals affecting integrity, efficiency, competitiveness, and stability of the U.S. financial markets."

What business, market, activity, or organization in the entire financial sector cannot be regulated, changed, or overridden in pursuit of "financial stability," "efficiency," and "competitiveness"? The answer is nothing and no one in the entire industry is outside the purview of Dodd-Frank. Just to list the headlined new agencies, regulatory powers, and responsibilities—for corporate governance, executive compensation, bank policies, credit agencies, hedge funds, financial advisors, and dozens more—requires a long paragraph. But such a list is almost irrelevant to the significance of Dodd-Frank: It arrogates to government unlimited power over the country's largest industry. And, commensurate with this power, commentators have pointed out, the new committee has a potentially unlimited budget and staff because it is authorized to call on the funds and personnel of dozens of huge government agencies. (A summary of the legislation is provided by Harvard Law School: http://blogs.law.harvard.edu/corpgov/2010/07/07/summary-of-dodd-frank-financial-regulation-legislation.)

The clear implication of Dodd-Frank is that if bureaucrats control everything, then no new crisis can develop. Of course: the premise that led to the legislation is that insufficient regulation permitted the 2008 crisis to occur. In a superb critique, called "Too Big Not To Fail," the *Economist* noted that the legislation is 848-pages long, but the section on the "Volcker rule," intended to prevent banks from taking excessive risks with their own (proprietary) trading and their investments in hedge funds, is a mere 11 pages. But five federal agencies responsible for making rules to implement that section "put forward a 298-page proposal which is, in the words of a banker publicly supportive of Dodd-Frank, 'unintelligible any way you read it'. It includes 383 explicit questions for firms which, if read closely, break down into 1,420 sub-questions."

To implement another section of just a few pages, two agencies issued "a form to be filled out by hedge funds and some other firms; that form ran to 192 pages. The cost of filling it out, according to an informal survey of hedge-fund managers, will be $100,000-150,000 for each firm the first time it does it. After having done it once, those costs might drop to $40,000 in every later year." (http://www.economist.com/node/21547784?fsrc=scn/tw/te/ar/toobignottofail.)

Get the point? If any matter, however small, is left unsupervised and unregulated by bureaucrats, something might go wrong. This was the wisdom of the Democratic majority in Congress in 2010—and, after all, what crisis did Congress ever precipitate—unless you count the national debt, runaway spending, crushing taxation, and "Obama care"?

Like every quantum leap in government power, Dodd-Frank became possible in an atmosphere of crisis—a crisis blamed on private enterprise in a climate of public fear, anger, and confusion. But, as we have discussed here, the causes of the crisis—not the particular nature of the mistakes, excesses, and shoddy dealings, but their scope, engulfing the entire U.S. economy and, indeed, the world— are found in the policies and actions of government over more than three decades. Therefore, the Dodd-Frank legislation makes the next crisis not less likely but virtually inevitable.

After all, what is there in Dodd-Frank to guard against the "financial instability" caused by virtually zero interest rates enforced year after year by the Fed? What will guard against the "financial instability" caused by trillions of dollars in new debt incurred since Mr. Obama became President? And what about the instability (i.e., inflation) inherent in "quantitative easing"? Or the instability caused by the Fed's manipulation of the stock market higher and higher without regard for the health of the economy? As Ayn Rand once asked: "Who Will Protect Us from Our Protectors?"

But is it "nationalization"?

Does this "great leap forward" in government involvement and control amount to nationalizing—socializing—the financial sector? The answer is technically, by definition, "no"—and, in fact, "yes."

The nationalizing of industry is the pivotal step in the move from capitalism to socialism. The transition to socialism never can be "peaceful" because the forcible expropriation of businesses, the violation of the property rights of thousands of citizens, is the primal act of violence at the birth of socialism. It is irrelevant whether or not the country voted to abandon property rights and expropriate owners; the massive violation remains. The only difference, perhaps, is that there is a special bitterness in knowing your fellow citizens consented at the polls to the seizure of your livelihood and wealth.

This is the literal implementation of socialism of one type, often called the "communistic" type. But economists, beginning with the great proponent of the Austrian School, Ludwig von Mises, have made a crucial distinction between two variants of socialism. One, as mentioned above, is the "communistic" type; the other is the "fascistic" type.

Use of the term "fascism" to describe a socialistic system once elicited looks of blank incomprehension; today, more people understand the term, though it never appears in the mainstream media. Socialism is the economic-political system under which the "means of production"—factories, mines, businesses, and other property—are owned by the government. But the essence of ownership is the right to use and disposal of property. If I "own" my factory, but the government makes all decisions about production, management, "profits" (if any), pay, and the price for which my output is sold, then my "ownership" is in name only. In fact, the government is the owner. Under fascism in Nazi Germany, factories, mines, and other businesses were not nationalized outright; the owners simply were told what to produce, in what quantities, at what price. This is socialism, and, of course, the full name of the Nazi Party was the National Socialist German Workers' Party. Benito Mussolini was long a member of the Italian Socialist Party and, in creating the Italian Fascist Party, was adding what he viewed as an element of Italian "patriotism" to socialism.

Fascism has been the pattern of statism's advance in the United States, a pattern identified by Ayn Rand in the early 1960s with her articles "The Fascist New Frontier" and "The New Fascism: Rule By Consensus." At that time, government command of the economy—at least as compared with today—was just beginning. The process has advanced and accelerated over more than half-a-century until, today, the mainstream *Economist* can speak of the "nationalization" of the largest business sector in the United States. "Nationalization" is rarely mentioned—just proposals to regulate, intervene, expropriate, and otherwise control the economy.

It is worth quoting the *Economist* as a summary of the trends I discussed, but also for the clear connection between crisis and government takeover. (Much of the analysis uses European examples; the nationalization of finance is not limited to the United States.)

"Each step taken by the authorities over the past five years has been designed to prop up the economy and save the financial system. But the cumulative effect has been the creeping nationalization of markets. Central banks are the biggest players in many rich-world government-bond markets. Equity markets seem to perk up only when central banks are expanding the money supply. And banking systems are incredibly reliant on implicit or explicit government support."

Reporting to Washington

Is the process of nationalization of finance complete? Of course not, but acceleration of the takeover since 2008 is frightening. Signs of a pervasive government assumption of control keep popping up. For example, government criticizes and, in some cases, sets the level of compensation for executives in businesses it "saved" with its largesse. And why not? Those executives are spending taxpayer dollars.

More recently, the media staged a circus in the aftermath of the estimated $2.0-billion trading loss taken by the prestigious Wall Street firm J. P. Morgan. Morgan had to announce the $2.0-billion loss, taken on European investments in "derivatives," just a week after its CEO, Jamie Dimon, in a call with reporters, indicated no knowledge of any problem. Dimon humbled himself in making the announcement of the loss, apologizing and taking blame, but that was not enough.

The loss, though significant by any standard, was nevertheless a small part of Morgan's huge reserve of capital and quarter after quarter Morgan had been reporting trading profits of about $4.0-billion. But the loss on the derivatives trade became a national issue. Mr. Dimon was summoned before Congress to explain how the loss could have occurred and spent hours responding to probes into and criticism of the firm's management and policies.

Morgan is, after all, a private firm, and investment firms do take losses—even large losses. And Morgan's record of trading had been consistently hugely profitable. Yet, Congress, the media, fellow financial executives, and, seemingly, Mr. Dimon, apparently saw nothing objectionable in his being called to Washington to explain himself and, in fact, fend off questions about why Morgan should not be taken over by government or "broken up."

A private firm in a private trade with its own capital, a loss that was large but less than its regularly profitable trading successes: was this a matter for government? Well, consider: In the 2008 financial panic, widely seen as threatening the entire world financial system, the core problem was identified as investment in "derivatives." Derivatives are financial instruments whose value is tied to the changing value of other securities, commodities, interest rates, or any of a host of other things. By the time of the financial panic, these derivatives held by financial firms ran into many trillions of dollars in "notional" value, the amount of money controlled by a relatively small investment (e.g., the insurance payable on a premium or, in the extreme, if all insurance holders had to be paid at the same time).

When the continued existence of a giant insurance firm, AIG, seemed doubtful, Wall Street firms like Morgan Stanley and Goldman Sachs quaked. AIG was the "counterparty" to a staggering total of derivatives that they held; if AIG went under those derivatives were suddenly worthless. Exactly what happened, and what would have happened given various scenarios, has been debated since 2008.

But Brian Pretti, one of today's outstanding independent economic and financial analysts, whose insights and predictions have consistently trumped those of most other analysts, does not hesitate to write: "Make no mistake about it, Goldman and Morgan Stanley would be distant memories, as would have a number of other leading US financial firms, had it not been for the Government bailout of the AIG derivatives debacle." That is a chilling statement from so careful and restrained a commentator as Mr. Pretti. It is worth reading all of Mr. Pretti's brilliant analysis (http://www.financialsense.com/contributors/brian-pretti/a-dimon-in-the-rough).

And so, since J.P. Morgan's "bad trade" was in derivatives, and since, today, after the harrowing escape from the financial crisis, the "notional value" of derivatives held by Morgan is $71.5 trillion (yes, seventy-one-and-a-half trillion dollars), far larger than the amount in 2008, is Morgan a "private firm" making private trades?

By the way, recall that the Fed exerts a crucial influence on the economy by manipulating interest rates. Today, thanks to the Fed, short-term interest rates are at the lowest level in history—effectively zero. And, for the first time, the Fed seeks to influence long-term rates, as well. With government's pervasive influence in this area, it should be obvious that interest rates could undergo a jolting change, almost overnight, should government change its policies. Is it any accident, then, that of the more than $225 trillion in "notional value" of derivatives held by the U.S. banking system, well over 95 percent are interest-rate derivatives? These are intended, say the banks, to "offset" most of their "interest-rate risk." This is the "financial-political complex" at work.

Can nationalization be stopped?

We know that once government is entrenched in a sector, then reversing that involvement, restoring freedom, is exceedingly difficult. How easy would it be, today, to get government out of the health care field—closing down or making private the Medicare and Medicaid programs? That's right, it seems impossible.

The same entrenchment is far advanced in the financial industry. What can be done? Rolling back government involvement will be enormously complex, but the essential steps are known and widely discussed by free-market economists.

First, the fuel of the America's financial engine is controlled by government. Government creates money and controls the amount of it in the economy. This represents the power to inflate (expand the money supply) at will and without limit. Government need not tax (and so face angry voters at the polls) or borrow. (After all, other countries, as well as businesses, compete to borrow money, and, at some point, lenders begin to worry that even the U.S. Government cannot repay the gigantic debt it has accumulated.) Government, though, can create money to buy its *own* debt, or, as during the financial crisis, to buy billions in private "toxic" assets.

If government were on a gold standard, as were most European governments and America throughout the Nineteenth Century and early Twentieth Century (and the United States partially so till 1971), it would be required to redeem its paper money in gold at a fixed rate. Its creation of money would be strictly limited, and, as in the Nineteenth Century, inflation would be a non-problem. Advocacy of a return to a gold standard is growing and increasingly vocal as government under the Obama administration creates and spends money like the proverbial drunken sailor. Return to the gold standard at a stroke would limit the size and power of government not only in the financial sector but the entire economy. (Although published in 1966, Alan Greenspan's essay, "Gold and Economic Freedom," is still the most succinct, philosophical, and persuasive case I know for a return to the gold standard. It is in Ayn Rand's book of essays, *Capitalism: The Unknown Ideal*. The Ludwig von Mises Institute also published a book by Ron Paul and Lewis Lehrman, *The Case for Gold* http://mises.org/daily/2826).

Second, the Federal Reserve Board is the locus of government control of money and credit, interest rates, and much of the regulation of the financial system. Its chairman has been called "the second most powerful person in government," after the President. Chairman Ben Bernanke, appointed by President George W. Bush, fits that description. He is an economics professor who believes that the Fed has unlimited responsibility for ensuring the stability and health of the economy.

In fact, the Fed's dual mandate is to maintain price stability and help to ensure full employment. It has tended to act mostly at times of recession, lowering interest rates to "stimulate" the economy, and then, when the economy begins to improve, raising rates supposedly to prevent inflation. This is not the place to evaluate the Fed's success; the point, here, is that, with the financial crisis, market crash, and recession, the Fed has arrogated to itself virtually total power to intervene in the financial system.

Principled advocates of *laissez-faire* capitalism call for abolishing the Fed, and the case is powerful. Like advocacy of the gold standard, however, calling for closing down the Fed is not an immediate (or even foreseeable) solution to the accelerating nationalizing of the financial sector. Still, many in Congress, and also commentators in the camp of free enterprise, oppose the growing power of the Fed and call for restraints. This could be an issue in the 2012 Presidential election if Mitt Romney called for limits on the Fed's role. Rep. Ron Paul, a Texas Republican and candidate for President, introduced legislation as early as 2002 to abolish the Fed and has kept pushing for it. His son, Sen. Rand Paul (R.-KY), is working to introduce legislation to increase government oversight of the Fed. (In 2009, Ron Paul published, *End the Fed*.)

Finally, remember that the problem is the "political-financial complex." That is, half the problem is with the financial sector. Wall Street, and the financial sector nationwide, can benefit—to the tune of billions of dollars in profits—from their "partnership" with government. I said earlier that the fortunes of the stock market are now tied to bouts of Fed "easing." Today, traders, investors, and the financial media focus obsessively on the prospect of the next Fed infusion of cash. To take another example, the Fed pumps money into banks, charging them negligible interest; the banks then invest in government bonds. They then collect interest from these virtually risk-free investments purchased with virtually free loans.

This is "crony capitalism" and must be exposed as such. In their "partnership" with government, financial firms are not earning profits by sound investment in open competition with others. They are benefiting from government largesse, favoritism, and guarantees. There is nothing "free" about this enterprise.

The battle against nationalization of the financial sector—a lunge toward socialism and guarantee of financial turmoil, including eventually runaway inflation, for years to come—is the battle for *laissez faire* capitalism itself. The case for free markets must be made on the economic level: for example, with demonstrations of the role of the Fed in causing the "boom and bust" cycle. But, above all, it must be made on the philosophical level, including insistence that seizure of control over the financial sector violates property rights as surely as "actual" nationalization. To seize effective control over private firms—the process now far advanced—is expropriation of the value of those firms even if they remain private in name. Right now, many firms are profiting from government intervention, but wait until the next, inevitable financial crisis, when the banks and brokers are declared to have failed utterly, endangering the economy, and we are told that the only answer is to nationalize them. Recall that as Congress questioned Mr. Dimon on the J.P. Morgan trading loss, they kept asking why Morgan should not be "broken up."

If the financial sector, Wall Street, once the epicenter of capitalism channeling investment to businesses nationwide and worldwide—the great marketplace where public companies are valued, bought, and sold—goes down before the onslaught of government's lust for power and control, then capitalism itself goes down.

Published *Financial Sense Online* May 19, 2012.

How to Explain the Crash to Your Barber
(September 2013)

It is going on five years since the financial panic that began in 2008 and cascaded into a stock market crash and depression. How many efforts have been made to explain to the public what happened? I started counting books about the crash on Amazon, 10 per page, and got through six pages before I stopped. Want to try to count the articles and editorials on the subject?

Going on five years, and the polls indicate that roughly half of American adults believe that Wall Street, bankers, and corporate CEOs were the cause—the villains. Period. My own experience is that, when pressed, these people get more specific about the cause: greed. A movie not worth naming, which is now playing in New York theaters, portrays an America destroyed by corporate greed until a committee of wise men restores control by sending out "bounty hunters" to kill corporate CEOs. Is that movie part of an emerging "folk wisdom" about the crash?

And so, advocates of economic freedom have failed to reach the public with the explanation of what really happened. Of course, some books made the problem worse, but books on the crash by Peter Schiff and Paul Volcker— to mention only two of many—were far from populist rabble rousing. I say "we" have failed because I penned two long articles about causes of the crash and panic that were hailed by a few dozen people who already agreed with me.

I think we have failed because we don't have a story: a narrative as blunt as the one that businessmen got carried away in a frenzy of greed and almost burned down the house.

Here, then, is my suggestion for telling the story.

Greed did not begin in 2005

Do not use any statistics, financial figures, or percentages when you tell this story. We all have more of those than we have money left in our 401Ks. Save them till you finish the story, save them for the question period.

You start the story by explaining that businessmen, bankers, and brokers have been greedy—that is, eager for profits—since caravans fought their way across barbaric lands to trade with China. Everywhere and always, the strong desire for profits—greed—motivates enterprise. Crucial point: You can't explain a once-in-a-hundred years financial panic (the previous one was 1907), a worldwide panic that almost burned down the house, by reference to a factor that always has existed. It isn't logical. It's dumb, but don't say that.

For the cause of a once-in-a-century event, we need more than ancient and omnipresent greed.

Now, why doesn't greed, and its inevitable excesses, regularly burn down the house? Think of an old-fashioned fuse box. Sometimes the current surges—sometimes lending gets sloppy and excessive, a new financial instrument becomes a craze, greedy but incompetent investors start taking on excess leverage—but the surge blows the fuse. Free markets are self-regulating.

Where only private capital is available, it is always limited. As more and more is demanded by too-greedy (incompetent) operators, interest rates rise. Capital gets scarce. And, yes, of course, the higher rates render some lousy investments unsustainable; businesses fail, brokers get no bonuses, some homeowners default on their mortgages. In other words, the current surges and the fuse blows. There is no more capital to feed the excess. Businesses and even industries suffer; but the house does not burn down.

I trust you have your listener's attention. Fuse, self-regulating, surges stopped early on, temporary blackout, but the house is saved. I know that by this point I had my wife's attention, and I have been trying to explain this for five years.

So what happened by late 2008? Another source of current suddenly had been flowing into the house—an outside source. And that source of current was unlimited. That source of investment capital was unlimited because it came from government. From a Federal Reserve that kept interest rates low no matter what the demand. From two government enterprises, the biggest mortgage agents in the world—Fannie Mae and Freddie Mac—that with government backing and special dispensation to "leverage-up" poured new mortgage money into the system.

The government had removed the fuses from the fuse box and replaced them with pennies, which no amount of current melts (not quite true, but good enough). Why? Because the flow of current gave the appearance of unlimited power, unlimited profits, bright light, a booming economy—happy voters, electable politicians. Why let the current blow a fuse and suffer perhaps a minor recession, or loss of profits for some companies? Just pull out the fuses, put in the pennies, and let the current flow.

This went on for years—decades, really—with at first an occasional recession (blown fuse); but each time the government responded by upping the current of capital and yanking another fuse.

By 2008, the permanent and unstoppable surge of current from the government—what we call "easy money," "easy credit," "monetary inflation"—had overloaded every appliance in the house, including some very shabby and flammable ones—and the house burst into flames.

The financial panic of 2008-2009, precipitating the stock market crash and depression, struck when the system simply could not absorb any more current—capital—and bankers, stockbrokers, and mortgage brokers flamed out. And in those flames, a huge amount of capital burned up, including part of your retirement savings and mine.

And that is the story

Bankers and brokers and speculators and homeowners and Wall Street giants had a role in the crash? Of course! They took advantage of the endless capital, the low interest rates, the largesse of Fannie and Freddie? Of course! Greedy, as always. As you and I are greedy about getting paid as much for our work as we can—but encounter the inevitable limits.

But ordinary greed, ancient greed, was enabled by government to soar to wild excesses. The self-limiting mechanisms of the market, the fuse box, was incapacitated.

The house that burned down was the private financial system, but the cause of the fire was government intervention. You can blame the homeowner because the house burned down—he played his part, for sure—but don't call him the necessary and sufficient cause. The cause was government.

This story, stripped of all statistics, all specific examples, is the sound skeleton of a new persona—the villain of the crash of 2008—that can be fleshed out with all our statistics, charts of money growth, historic context, and macro-economic analysis. That persona will rise and walk because it has a powerful skeleton.

This story has the virtue of being true, but also of stating our case in the most essential terms. Your barber will understand it even if he doesn't assent at the moment.

I tell you that with confidence. Because when I finished telling this story to my wife, she did not say, as she has for five years, "You know I don't understand all that stuff."

She said, "How come people don't see this?"

And, after a moment, she added: "You ought to write that, so people will get it.

Published on *Financial Sense* on September 19, 2013.

Bernie, Bernie: Was It 'Selfish'?
(December 2010)

Many would say Bernard Madoff was a very selfish man—a man who hurt others, including his own family, because he acted only for himself. But did he?

Madoff announced yesterday, through his lawyer, that he will not attend the funeral of his oldest son, Mark Madoff, 46, who committed suicide over the weekend. Mark hung himself in his Soho apartment in New York City, using a dog leash slung over a pipe. He left his second wife, his two-year-old daughter, and also a previous family that includes two grown children.

A father ordinarily might wish to attend the funeral of his oldest son, but Bernard Madoff is serving a 150-year prison sentence for perpetrating the largest, most damaging (non-governmental) Ponzi scheme investment fraud in history, which devastated the lives of thousands of investors who trusted him. If he attended his son's funeral, his presence would create a media circus of epic proportions, turning the funeral into a horror show for Mark Madoff's wife and baby daughter and other family members, including Bernard Madoff's wife.

It was the firestorm of anger and hate for the very Madoff name, and also an endless stream of lawsuits, criminal and civil, that drove Mark Madoff to kill himself on the second anniversary of his father's arrest for the legendary Ponzi scheme. The same vehement notoriety caused Bernard Madoff's wife to petition a court to change her name and the name of her two children from Madoff to something — anything—else.

As Bernard Madoff's various homes, boats, and other possessions, including even his shoes, have been auctioned off to raise a few dollars to help compensate his victims, his name has become synonymous with dishonesty—the very embodiment of ugly immorality. Given the sentence he received, he will die in jail, but this is viewed as inadequate punishment for his crimes.

Our culture has one virtually universally agreed-upon term for Bernard Madoff's behavior: "selfish."

That was the motivation, was it not, of this man who ruthlessly devastated the lives of so many people, so many friends, family members, and associates who trusted him with their savings?

"He acted only for himself"

He acted only for himself; and, we have been taught, selfish behavior in all its forms is the cardinal moral danger to the social order. To act merely for oneself, one's own values, goals, interests, implies a possible range of behavior from merely mean to monstrous. Given no principle but selfishness to guide behavior, there supposedly are no limits to destructiveness. Hence Bernard Madoff.

But this brief description of Bernard Madoff's life, today, raises an obvious question: How did behavior motivated solely by concern for self, for his own self-interest, lead to the life he now lives—and will live until his death behind bars?

He has nothing of his own, save personal effects in his prison cell. His wife seeks only to sever herself from his name. His eldest son timed his suicide to mark the anniversary of Bernard Madoff's arrest and public disgrace, and Madoff himself is viewed as such a fascinating object of loathing and morbid curiosity that he dare not attend his son's funeral.

Bernard Madoff was and is a brilliant man. He created and maintained a mind-bogglingly complex scheme of deception that over decades fooled government regulators, bankers, brokers, and investment professionals of every kind—as well as his associates, closest friends, and family. He built an empire based on out-witting all comers in one of the most scrutinized and competitive businesses in the world. If he set his mind to pursuing only his self-interest, his own values and fulfillment, how could he have gone so completely, disastrously wrong?

Posed this way, the question has no satisfactory answer. The problem, I think, is with one of our assumptions. Before we accept the assumption that Bernard Madoff acted selfishly, we should pose a commonsense test. If we were in young Bernard Madoff's shoes, beginning his career, what would be some obvious selfish goals? To be plain and perhaps unimaginative: to earn lots of money to obtain and enjoy comforts, such as luxurious apartments, and pleasures, such as travel, vacation homes, boats—and to enjoy these acquisitions in peace.

Perhaps to marry an attractive woman (he did) who would love us and admire us, and to have children who would admire us and make us proud by succeeding in their own right. To enjoy the admiration and friendship of colleagues and friends. Simple and obvious things—and nary a mention of what are deemed unselfish pursuits, such as philanthropy, service to our fellow men, religious piety, or sacrifice for supposed ideals such as public service, patriotism, making a better world.

But I would suggest that Bernard Madoff, by any common reckoning, pursued none of those selfish values. He did not earn money, he stole it; and, although he acquired many possessions, he hardly could have enjoyed them in anything like peace and serenity, given his constant vigilance, scheming, deception, and manipulation. And, of course, he lost everything and is spending what should be his years of achievement and satisfaction in a medium-security federal prison.

Did he enjoy the admiration and love of his wife, given what he knew all along about the life he had created for her? And what do any years in which she did love and admire him mean now, as she seeks to disown his very name? His sons, his friends, his colleagues? He did not in fact pursue any of these values; he pursued the pretense of them: the appearance of achievement, the misguided love and admiration of wife, sons, and friends. He pursued not one real value, not one real interest of the self.

The vanishing self

I would suggest to you that Bernard Madoff pursued only an image in the minds of others: the image of a successful businessman, the image of a caring husband and father, the image of the creator of wealth and plenty, the image of a man on top of the world. He was not selfish; he created a life in which his existence was solely in the deluded minds of others.

Bernard Madoff's "self" was a mere misapprehension in other minds. When he dies, nothing real will die. Whatever existed will continue to exist in the minds of others—but now as an avatar of contemptible and ultimately pathetic futility.

Bernard Madoff is a very selfless man.

And we should be very, very afraid of unselfish men.

_____

Published on *The Atlasphere* on December 16, 2010.

U.S. Economic Freedom: Retreat Becomes Rout
(September 2012)

Measurement is often the crucial step in understanding—and gaining control—of a complex phenomenon. For example, we debate—endlessly, it seems—the state of economic freedom in America. But the Fraser Institute, a Canadian think tank, gives us the crucial ability to go beyond that. Since 1996, with a project inspired by the late Milton Friedman, the Institute has published an extraordinarily sophisticated report that measures the economic freedom of every major country in the world—and tracks the rise or decline of freedom in each country—so that we can talk about *how much, in what areas,* and *to what effect.*

Their report, released yesterday, is *Economic Freedom of the World in 2010.* Let me give you the bottom line for the United States of America—which we have called, and rightly so, a "beacon to the world" when it comes to economic freedom and the prosperity it makes possible. In the words of the report ("Chain-linked" simply refers to a method that ensures the study, when measuring changes over time, is comparing apples to apples):

"The United States, long considered the standard bearer for economic freedom among large industrial nations, has experienced a substantial decline in economic freedom during the past decade. From 1980 to 2000, the United States was generally rated the third freest economy in the world, ranking behind only Hong Kong and Singapore. After increasing steadily during the period from 1980 to 2000, the chain-linked EFW [*Economic Freedom of the World*] rating of the United States fell from 8.65 in 2000 to 8.21 in 2005 and 7.70 in 2010. The chain-linked ranking of the United States has fallen precipitously from second in 2000 to eighth in 2005 and 19th in 2010..."

America's decline over just one decade was from the third most economically free nation in the world to the nineteenth. What does this mean, in practice? The report measures economic freedom in five broad areas: size of government, legal system and property rights, sound money, freedom to trade internationally, and regulation. Within these categories, however, this painstaking report measures 42 variables. Or, as the Institute puts it in still broader terms, economic freedom is made up of four key ingredients: personal choice, voluntary exchange, freedom to compete, and security of privately owned property.

This is what we are talking about losing, at a rate the Institute calls "precipitous," since the beginning of the new century in 2000. (You may or may not be consoled to know that over the past two years average economic freedom in the world at large increased very slightly.) The United States is among the four countries in the world with the largest decline in economic freedom since 2000. The others are Venezuela, Argentina, and Iceland. We now trail even Bahrain, the United Arab Emirates, Estonia, Taiwan, and Qatar.

The rating assigned to United States economic freedom has declined in four of the five broad areas listed above. The only area where the United States held its own, until 2010, was access to sound money (not to say that the situation was good, only that it was no worse than in 2000, since the "quantitative easing" by the Fed was just beginning, back then).

What we are losing

What is actually happening within these categories? Let's look at one in which the U.S. experienced the sharpest decline: "Legal System and Protection of Property Rights." Among the specific losses of freedom were the increased use of eminent domain to transfer private property for the benefit of politically backed projects, ramifications of the wars on terror and drugs, and violation of the rights of bondholders in the bailout of the automotive companies.

If you are among those who feel that economic freedom is over-rated and perhaps even undesirable (Mr. Obama might fall into this category, for example), realize that scholarly studies show that a one point decline in economic freedom hits long-term economic growth, reducing it between 1.0 and 1.5 percentage points annually. The Fraser report says: "This implies that, unless policies undermining economic freedom are reversed, the future annual growth of the US economy will be half its historic average of 3%."

You could spend many profitable hours with this report, and economic researchers and scholars do just that, launching study after study based on the report's data—and especially the invaluable longitudinal, cumulative data. A few conclusions of these studies may suggest the importance of the *Economic Freedom of the World Report*:

"All studies have shown that countries with policies most consistent with economic freedom have higher investment rates, more rapid economic growth, higher income levels, and a higher reduction in poverty rates.

"In the top one-quarter of countries with most economic freedom, the average income of the poorest 10 percent of the population was about $11,400; in the bottom quartile it was about $1,200. The report adds that the average income of the poorest 10 percent of people in the economically freest countries is more than twice the *average* income in the least free countries.

"Life expectancy is about 80 years in the top quartile of countries by economic freedom; in the bottom quartile, it is 62 years.

"Political and civil liberties correlate very closely with the economic freedom of a country."

These are bare summaries of conclusions based on data and research that you can review in depth in the Fraser report here: http://www.freetheworld.com/2012/EFW2012-complete.pdf.

The inestimable contribution of the Fraser Institute report is to add to the case for economic freedom an element of careful measurement of the destructiveness of policies (supposedly well-motivated) that curtail economic freedom and the literally life-giving benevolence of policies that leave us free to choose, compete, trade, and keep, and enjoy the rewards of our work.

Published *The Atlas Society* September 9, 2012.

"A Buck for Your Thoughts"

Don't take it! Hold out for at least $3.25!
(November 2014)

If your sweetheart murmurs, "A penny for your thoughts," reply, "Yeah, if this were 500 years ago."

It was almost 500 years ago that the English divine, Thomas More, now St. Thomas More, wrote, in 1522, in an essay entitled "Four Last Things":

"It often happeth, that the very face sheweth the mind walking a pilgrimage, in such wise that other folk sodainly say to them a peny for your thought."

Could the English penny in 1522 purchase what a dollar purchases today? There are many measurements of the changing value of money, but one site puts the value of one British penny in 1522 at $3.35 in 2013 (http://eh.net/howmuchisthat).

A "penny," a "quarter," and a "dollar" are just words. Today, they are words with no fixed meaning—or a meaning that changes day by day. For example, today, November 3, the U.S. dollar rose to an almost seven-year high in its exchange rate with the Japanese yen. In the foreign exchange markets, since May, the dollar has soared in value almost 10 percent against a basket of other foreign currencies.

The value of the dollar you carry in your pocket everywhere, every day, and all your life is anchored to *nothing*. This was not always the case.

So much has been written about money, its nature, and its vexed relationship to "real value"—and about the mighty U.S. dollar—that one must cut, slash, through to a few essentials. Let me borrow that most hackneyed of titles:

Ten Things to Know About the Dollar

Since 1913, when the U.S. Government nationalized control of our currency, the U.S. dollar has lost at least 97 percent of its purchasing power. Roughly, what you could buy for one dollar in 1913 costs about $20, now. If you earned a dollar in 1913 and kept it in a drawer, today it would be worth about three cents. What happened in 1913? The federal government created the Federal Reserve System, a central committee and network of banks that, in effect, took over control of money, which, until then, had been created by the states or by banks, a largely private matter.

The value of the dollar did not always erode year after year. During much of the Nineteenth Century, the dollar held its value—or gained value. Because every dollar at any time could be exchanged, at a set rate, for gold, banks could not create money unless they had gold to back it—and the amount of gold on average increases very slowly. Thus, the productivity of the country, the amount of goods produced, grew much faster than the amount of gold or gold-backed dollars—so prices tended to fall.

Creation of the Federal Reserve System was justified as a way to prevent financial panics, like the great panic of 1907, but within less than 20 years, the Fed had created a financial bubble that burst in 1929, bringing on the Great Depression. In 2007, after two decades that were the most active in the history of the Fed, the United States plunged into the worst financial panic in its history. The Fed had sought to maintain a permanent prosperity, with no recessions, by constantly enlarging the money supply: much of this went into the real estate, banking, and investment sectors—those that precipitated the financial panic, crash, and a global depression.

In 1933, the new administration of Franklin Delano Roosevelt took the country off the gold standard, abrogated contracts written in terms of gold, and made it a crime for any U.S. citizen or company to own ("hoard") gold. All gold had to be sold to the government for $20.67 an ounce (it had remained at that price for 100 years). It was probably the first time in all history that people lost the right to own gold. The Roosevelt administration ended the gold standard so that the government could print new dollars without needing gold to back them. The theory was that giving Americans more "purchasing power" would get the economy out of the Great Depression. It didn't; but each new dollar printed to give someone "purchasing power" reduced the value of dollars already in the hands of people who earned them. The great debasement of the dollar began.

Beginning in 1933, when government seized the power to print new dollars unbacked by gold—or anything—the U.S. dollar has lost value steadily for 80 years. Of course, there have been intermediate fluctuations. Since May, about six months, the U.S. dollar has gained purchasing power against a basket of foreign currencies that make up the U.S. Dollar Index. Chief among those currencies are the Euro, Yen, and Swiss franc. This temporary rise has resulted entirely because of political decisions, especially those of the Fed, which finally announced cessation of the largest money-creating spree in history.

U.S. citizens who watch the value of the U.S. dollar, and their savings, shrinking year after year cannot refuse to accept dollars. Our legal tender laws make the dollar "legal tender for all debts public and private." If I owe you $1,000 and offer to pay in dollars you cannot refuse; you cannot, for example, demand payment in gold.

Some 80 years of money creation (inflation) has not destroyed acceptability of the dollar abroad–not entirely–because at the height of American power after World War II, in 1946, the governments of the world agreed at the Bretton Woods conference to accept the U.S. dollar as the world's official reserve currency and standard of exchange. That's right: Other nations are required to accept the U.S. dollar in international exchange, and, for example, all purchases of oil and other energy are in dollars and central banks hold much of their foreign reserves in dollars. The United States agreed, in turn, to exchange the dollar for gold at a fixed rate (an offer to other nations but not to American citizens).

In 1971, the United States broke this promise to foreign nations to exchange dollars for gold. The Fed had created more and more dollars and the dollar had lost value; the world economy, and especially Europe, had been flooded with dollars. The United States simply didn't have enough gold in Fort Knox to keep its promise. Since 1971, in particular, inflation in the United States and much of the world—the debasement of the dollar's value—have accelerated hugely.

Despite the United States' breaking its side of the bargain (to exchange dollars for gold), the U.S. dollar has remained the world's official exchange and reserve currency; but foreign nations now are in active rebellion against this. No longer required to have gold to back the dollar, even in international exchange, the dollar had lost the last anchor of its value. Money creation by the Fed soared, and, since 1971, the value of the dollar has plunged. Other nations holding dollars, which they were paid for their goods and services, and used as bank reserves, watched the value of the dollar—and their foreign reserves—shrink year by year. They are rebelling. Both

China and Russia, for example, have now secured agreements with groups of nations to conduct exchanges in ways that bypass the dollar. China today is the world's largest purchaser of gold, using its huge earnings from sales to the United States and Europe. Most observers believe that China's goal is to supplant the U.S. dollar with the yuan as the world's official exchange currency.

In 1975, yielding to public protest, the U.S. government again permitted its citizens to own gold— but not to use it as a medium of exchange. During the period that gold had been a strict government monopoly, there had been an official gold price: $35 an ounce. But when Americans could buy and sell gold, exchanges in the open market set the gold price. Between 1975 and today, the price of gold in dollars has risen from $35 to about $1200 an ounce. For thousands of years, gold has been a yardstick of the "real" value of paper money created and manipulated by governments. The price of an ounce of gold since 1975 has increased 3,400 percent. Gold has not become more valuable relative to other real goods; the entire change in price results from the dollar's precipitous loss of value.

In another decade, you may get 10 bucks for your thoughts. But they be pretty gloomy.

Published on *The Savvy Street* on November 16, 2014.

Speak, Switzerland!
(October 2014)

In the United States, if we hold a referendum, so voters may speak directly and decisively on a question, it always is at the state level, and, lately, most often addresses the legality of gay marriage, the decriminalization of marijuana, getting tough on illegal immigrants, or some other grave matter.

You never will guess what the Swiss, by giving more than 100,000 signatures in support of a Swiss People's Party referendum, will be deciding in a nationwide vote on November 30. They will vote on whether or not the Swiss National Bank (the equivalent of the U.S. Federal Reserve) should be prohibited from selling its precious metals, including gold; should be required to hold at least 20 percent of its foreign reserves in gold; and should hold its gold within the country.

Can you imagine a more gnomish matter? It seems that just 10 years ago, the Swiss National Bank (SNB) had the highest per capita gold holdings in the world. And the Swiss liked it that way. But, taking advantage of a time when the world economy was calm and prosperity comfortable, Switzerland in a national referendum in 1999 authorized the bank to sell 50 percent of its gold reserves. Through 2008, the bank sold hundreds of tons of gold—always too cheaply, because the price of gold kept climbing.

The chairman of the SNB's board of directors declared that having a currency (the Swiss Franc) backed 40 percent by gold was "a relic." And so it was, in one sense. When the U.S. Federal Reserve Bank was created in 1913, the U.S. dollar was backed 40 percent by gold. Imagine, Switzerland not catching up after all these years!

Except that the Swiss Franc, backed by gold, has tended to sustain its purchasing power over the decades. Whereas the U.S. dollar, since creation of the Federal Reserve, has lost at least 95 percent of its value. Probably more. At times of crisis, such as 2008, foreign investors have rushed to convert their dollars, or Euros, or pesos into Swiss francs. The result has been to push up the value of the Swiss franc against other currencies. Sometimes by a lot—25 percent against the U.S. dollar, at one point.

Conventional banker's wisdom is that this is bad for exports. Swiss goods denominated in francs are pricey against the wimpy dollar or Euro. Furthermore, a currency heavily backed by gold makes its almost impossible for a central bank to depreciate the currency—that is, to print more money, to inflate. And such "expansion of the money supply," goes the conventional wisdom of central bankers, can be crucial in stimulating an economy. (Critics say that, yes, it stimulates the economy, creates burgeoning bad investments, or "bubbles," and then, when the money drug no longer can be supplied in ever-greater quantities, the economy crashes. Boom and bust. You know, like the real-estate bubble and crash of 2008.)

But we won't be able to manipulate money!

The SNB and the Swiss government are campaigning fiercely for defeat of the referendum. Their argument is that approval of the referendum will limit the flexibility of the SNB to manipulate the quantity of money to stimulate the economy and encourage exports. The argument of those that support the referendum is a mirror image of this: requiring a Swiss franc heavily backed by gold will prevent the SNB from manipulating the money supply and inflating the currency. It's all in your viewpoint.

Right now, Switzerland holds about 1040 metric tons of gold, about 7.8 percent of its foreign reserves, so you see that the "relic" of 40 percent gold reserves against the franc is no more. The referendum, if approved—and it is gaining support, to the dismay of the Keynesian money crowd—would require the bank approximately to triple its reserves over the next five years. Depending on prices, that is as much as $83 billion in gold purchases (gold and gold-mining stock investors are paying attention).

If the course of the Swiss referendum is typical, then about October 21, a week or so before the vote, the slugging match over the referendum will become violent. At this point, perhaps the story of this decision and its significance will surface, if only fleetingly, in international news sources. So far, the referendum has been reported only in a few financial publications.

In the United States, the virtually limitless power of the Federal Reserve to create hundreds of billions of new money out of thin air has become a political matter. In fact, there is a disturbingly good case that the Federal Reserve's money expansion in the nick of time saved the stock market long enough to hand Barrack Obama re-election. There are bills or proposals in the U.S. Congress to limit the power of the "Fed"—or even close it down.

Imagine how much simpler, and more appealing, might be legislation to require the Federal Reserve to back the issuance of all new money with a 20 percent reserve of gold. "Keep the U.S. dollar as good as gold." "Restore the integrity of dollar." "Turn soft-headed thinking into hard money!" "Make a dollar worth a dollar, again!"

Imagine what a brilliant publicist could do if he had an understanding that our national prosperity, and even our civil peace, may depend upon clawing back control over our money. Remember, it was the great German inflation between the world wars that broke the German middle class and left it open to the inflammatory calls for "revenge" by history's deadliest demagogue.

Speak, Switzerland!

Note: On November 30, 2014, Swiss voters defeated the "Save Our Swiss Gold" proposal with 78 percent voting against it.

Published on *Financial Sense* in October 21, 2014.

The Theme Song Is "Yuan the Mighty Dragon"
(October 2013)

I wonder if, watching the clamorous melodrama in the United States Congress over the budget and debt, the American public and world could miss the sound track—the theme song—playing in the background? Both sides in the clash were loudly strumming the same song, but singing different words. Don't try to decipher the words, listen to the tune.

From different perspectives, I think, both sides foresee the coming perfect storm when exponentially ballooning spending; the Fed's utterly unprecedented monetary inflation; and the debt that we as a nation have created simply cannot be sustained any longer on the life support of: 1) the Federal Reserve's creating most of the money, now, to "buy" U.S. bonds—buying our own debt with new dollars we create, and, 2) the Fed pressing short-term interest rates near to zero, year after year, so that interest on the gigantic U.S. debt burden is sustainable—for now.

Over decades, the champions of government power and dominance (statists) in both parties have put the U.S.

economy, the financial balance sheet of government, and the country's credit in such a fantastically (literally "fantasy") dangerous and fragile position—aborting every free-market correction with the panacea of more borrowing and inflation—that today those who say that to put the country's credit in default, to halt the Fed's inflation, to rein-in government spending would lead to catastrophe are right. They are correct in a much deeper way than they themselves may understand.

By now, we are far too deep in the credit-expansion cycle to halt without precipitating a crash and deep depression. That is reality; we have bought and paid for it, and now see the battle between those who would begin to face it and those who would postpone facing it until it smashes down on us despite all interventions. The Tea Party might unleash at last the perfect storm that always is the end game of government-induced (and prolonged, and PROLONGED) boom. (Although the current drawn-out life-support for the economy is now as much "boom" as trillions in quantitative easing can achieve.) There will be bust and it will be horrendous, revealing the actual state of the economy and government's long overdue admission of bankruptcy.

I don't think that the Tea Party understands or intends to release that storm, which, inevitably, must strike. They want to halt the plunge deeper into the credit maelstrom. But, as we know from von Mises and others, there is no mere halting; not to continue to expand credit is to bring about the bust. Indeed, everything government has done in the past six years has loudly acknowledged the fragility of the system.

Do you hear the theme song? Borrowed money, creating money to buy our own bonds, manipulating interest rates to leash the potentially explosive interest payments on burgeoning debt: borrow money, create money, juggle debt... Do you hear the theme song of the future? It is: phony money versus real money.

The real money

While Congress and President Obama, the press, and world's bankers are cheering or booing or moaning about the United States' phony-money melodrama, who in the world wants real money? Who will hold the real money when the *Great Credit and Borrowing and Bluffing Charade* simply collapses—and with it the U.S. dollar?

Well, real money, for at least the past 5000 years, has been gold. Is that old hat? Central banks all over the globe have halted—stopped—their selling their gold holdings and started saving and rebuilding them. Central banks. Real money.

And the price of gold since about 2001 has risen from about $250 an ounce to $1900 an ounce in 2011, without a single year in which the price failed to rise. Since 2011, it has corrected, falling to $1,300 an ounce—still about five times what it was a decade ago. Why has gold finally corrected, now, as the perfect storm brews? Because the Fed has deliberately, and by announcement, created a tsunami of newly created money to bolster the stock market and promote equities (risk), and this tsunami has gone on so long and so consistently that investors now think the stock market never will stop making new highs. And so money has flowed out of the huge gold-holding Exchange Traded Funds (ETFs) into the stock market. Gold is having a brief clearance sale because for now the Fed's unlimited power to create phony money has mesmerized stock market investors.

Who has come to that sale to take advantage of the bargain? Who is buying gold? No country in the world comes CLOSE to matching the gold purchases that will be made this year alone by China. China, by the end of the year—adding in its purchases and its own mined gold (no mined gold leaves China)—will have added 1700 tons of gold to its reserves. How much is 1700 tons in one year? Well, the total U.S. gold holdings in Fort Knox and elsewhere, accumulated over the American Republic's entire history, is 8033 tons.

In one year, China has purchased gold equal to 21 percent of total U.S. gold holdings. And those purchases have not dented China's free foreign reserves of $1.3 trillion.

As the U.S. Congress and President Obama are locked in farcical combat over phony money—debt, borrowing, and inflation—China is accumulating tons of real money.

China wants a new world agreement; it has called for a new Bretton Woods agreement, which, after World War II, made the U.S. dollar the world's official reserve currency because it then was backed by gold. And now? If the U.S. sold its gold holdings, in total, at today's price, it would produce enough to meet U.S. government expenditures for one month. Right, one month.

China will accumulate enough gold to back its currency and, as all of economic history shows, will become an irresistible magnet for the world's savings, the world's credit, and the world's fiduciary trust. The world's trade and bank reserves will be in the Chinese Yuan.

On our present course, this will not be long in coming. China watches our politicians and the Fed slipping into a deeply subjective and unreal world. It watches and prepares. To wait a decade or even two is nothing. The ancient Dragon Throne has time.

_____

Published *Financial Sense Online* October 17, 2013.

Just another Successful Businessman— Destroyed: The Ordeal of Greg Reyes
(August 2012)

Quite long ago, Whittaker Chambers wrote: "The great failing of American conservatives is they don't retrieve their wounded." That bitter reflection, but as applied to American businessmen, came to mind when I finished reading the story of Greg Reyes.

Reyes, a second-generation Cuban immigrant, rose through sheer talent, productivity, and vision to become, at 36, the CEO of Brocade Communications—a Silicon Valley company that revolutionized computer-storage technology (and whose revenues he increased twenty-fold in three years). Not long after, he found himself sentenced to prison, his wealth destroyed, his career and life blown to bits.

The crime of which he was convicted was the violation of a complex accounting regulation. The prosecution, even by advertising nationally, could find no investor who could assert coherently that the "misstated" information had any impact on his investment decisions.

But there *must* be more to it than that! I will offer two answers to that very understandable reaction. First, there was (you *do* remember?) the backdated options frenzy stirred up, beginning in 2005, by story after story in the *Wall Street Journal*, stories that only rarely mentioned that backdating options was *not* illegal and was practiced by hundreds of Silicon Valley companies, but spent paragraph after paragraph talking about corporate greed and describing the homes, cars, vacations, and other luxuries of the wealthy. In this case, anti-capitalist journalism led and set the pace for Securities and Exchange Commission enforcement and Justice Department prosecutions.

And, second, yes, there is more: And the "more" is *more* strained and incredible than the fact that accounting rule APB 25 was used by the SEC and prosecutors to destroy billions of dollars in the value of companies, lay waste executive careers, and put in prison—as examples or scapegoats—just five executives from the thousands of companies that "restated" company earnings when APB 25 was "clarified."

The "class warfare" President

There is a context, here, without which the backdated options frenzy and the stop-at-nothing drive-by prosecutions to put Greg Reyes in jail makes no sense. In a recent article, David Stockman, the famous first Office of Management and the Budget Director under Ronald Reagan, charged that President Barrack Obama has appealed to class-warfare, resentment of the financially successful, more than any other Democratic president since FDR.

It is not just Mr. Obama. In fact, Reyes was indicted in 2006, during the Bush administration. But Mr. Obama is the quintessential product of a generation that emerged from college, law school or business school imbued with a crusading spirit against the supposed social destructiveness, immorality, and unfairness of capitalism—as personified by the most successful, wealthy entrepreneurs, businessmen, and, in particular, financiers.

We have seen this played out, again and again, by the waves of moral outrage against a particular businessman, or business practice, which is whipped up by ambitious crusading reporters and given a sense of legitimacy by government prosecutors. There have been genuine criminals in the business world, of course; few men have destroyed as much wealth, and hurt so many lives, by sheer fraud, as Bernard Madoff. But for every Bernard Madoff, whose crimes are clear and specific, there are dozens of businessmen of towering achievement such as Michael Milken and Frank Quattrone whose supposedly terrible deeds very few recall, except for the vague impression that they did something "awful."

Such victims of media "rich-hunt" and prosecutorial ambition—in truth, victims of a political ideology and animus—rarely have many defenders. The moment a businessman, a financial firm, is reported to be "under investigation" or about to be indicted, the individual or firm is isolated, instantaneously "on trial." The repeated pattern of politically and ideologically motivated crusades, energized by reporters hungry for the great expose, seems to matter little. Each time, the attention of the world is arrested by the new outrage.

Several years ago, the Atlas Society, a Washington, D.C., nonprofit organization of which I am a trustee, decided that it was time to fight for some balance. The Atlas Society created a Business Rights Center to bring facts, perspective, and tough analysis to the ever-more-frequent attacks on businessmen. The Center seeks out the facts and context of allegations against business, but, in particular, it focuses on individual businessmen who become "stars" of the media-prosecution dramas.

Not Half Free: The Myth that America is Capitalist

Exposing the expose

As the prosecution of individuals such as Greg Reyes ground on—long after the *Wall Street Journal* had finished riding the backdated options story, and few knew what happening in court, or why—the director of the Business Rights Center, Roger Donway, began two years of intensive research on the backdated options story. (Full disclosure: I am a trustee of the Atlas Society and Roger Donway is my brother.) The result, published last month by the Atlas Society, is *Rich-Hunt: The Backdated Options Frenzy and the Ordeal of Grey Reyes* (The Atlas Society, Washington, DC: 2012, 159 pages.) The book is the most carefully researched, detailed, and extensively documented report on both the issue and the scarcely believable experience of Greg Reyes with the "criminal justice" system.

The facts, context, and arguments (including the arcane aspects of some three decades of struggle by various accounting bodies to clarify the reporting requirements for backdated options) are presented with the utmost clarity in the book. I will not repeat them here. What the reader needs to know is that this book also has the drama, pace, and moral tension of a John Grisham novel. I will suggest that very few readers who don't bring to the book the attitude that all-businessmen-succeed-by-hurting-people will come away without a shudder at what government regulators and prosecutors will do to bring down their man.

The first trial of Greg Reyes ended in conviction. The prosecutor pushed for a prison sentence of 30 years, a fine of $41 million, and "restitution" of $90 million. Greg Reyes contemplated suicide. On appeal, the Ninth Circuit Court ruled that the prosecutor had lied and called for retrial. The *same* prosecutor was assigned to the second trial—and word leaked out that the U.S. Attorney blamed Reyes for "staining the honor" of his office and vowed revenge. The second trial mounted an entirely different attack on Reyes, one that directly contradicted the allegations made in the first trial. The baffled court said, "Let me make sure I understand. Because this is the first time I have heard this argument in three years…"

Prison for defrauding…no one

Greg Reyes was again convicted, and sentenced to 18 months in prison and a fine of $15,000.000. Although he was convicted of fraud, no evidence ever was advanced that any investor was hurt or had made any different decision about investing in Brocade because of the accounting misstatement. How could they have been misled? All the information was stated, just not in the form apparently required ("apparently" because accountants never could agree on it) by APB 25. *Who* was defrauded? No answer. Nor did the prosecutor show, at any time, that Reyes himself benefited from the backdating.

But by then, Reyes, after six years of hellish uncertainty, had demanded that he begin to serve his sentence—to get it over with, to get some certainty, to get some closure. His appeal to the Circuit Court of the second conviction was denied. The Supreme Court refused to hear the case.

He is now out on probation, barred from ever pursuing an ambition he had from the age of 12 to be a Silicon Valley CEO, barred by a settlement with the SEC from ever denying his guilt—on pain of re-imprisonment—and stripped of most of his fortune by the fine, the gigantic costs of his legal defense, and a huge settlement extracted by Brocade based on his conviction.

Greg Reyes now has no way to seek restoration of his reputation, no way to seek justice—the legal system has spoken. He has only the verdict of history, which, though it comes slowly, is final. And that is a verdict that depends upon you, and me, and anyone who takes the time to read *Rich-Hunt: The Backdated Options Frenzy and the Ordeal of Greg Reyes*. It is time that those who understand that America's greatness is inseparable from its commitment to capitalism, and that the heroes of our time are the entrepreneurs and the other great wealth-creators, retrieved our wounded.

Published *Financial Sense Online*, August 15, 2012.

Obama's Power Move: Scapegoating Speculators
(April 2012)

On April 17, 2012, President Barrack Obama addressed Americans about the rising price of gasoline, now above $5.00 a gallon in parts of the country. In any market economy, the cause of rising prices is that demand for a product has increased relative to the supply of it. Prices come down when demand is reduced or supply increased. That these obvious principles must be repeated is part of the problem we face.

President Obama, standing beside his attorney general (suggesting the tenor of his "solution"), gave a brief nod to "supply and demand"—and then got to this proposal for pretending that they are irrelevant. His proposal is to spend $52 million to regulate, suppress, and punish "speculators" who allegedly are causing higher prices at the pump by "manipulating" the oil price.

He proposed a ten-fold increase in civil and criminal penalties for "illegal manipulation" of oil prices, but did not define such manipulation. Indeed, the proposal appears to call for spending money to ascertain what "manipulation" *is*. My best guess is that what is being targeted is investment money from large institutions that are buying oil in anticipation of a rise in prices.

Not Half Free: The Myth that America is Capitalist

The speech was cast in Mr. Obama's rhetoric of pitting the American middle class against the wealthy: "We can't afford a situation where some speculators can reap millions while millions of American families get the short end of the stick." Marxist class-warfare rhetoric has evolved, in recent years, from references to "the poor" and "disadvantaged" to the middle class because that is where the votes are. Also, the policies of ever-greater regulation, taxation, and inflation threaten the prosperity of the middle class, making their fears ripe for political exploitation and scapegoating.

What speculators do

It is embarrassing to hear the President of what is, for all its burden of government controls, still seen as a great capitalist country, blaming speculators for economic consequences caused by supply and demand, and, to a considerable extent, by government. The speculators to whom Mr. Obama refers are traders in the futures markets, who buy or sell contracts for future delivery of a host of commodities—including crude oil. Their sole objective is to discern the direction of prices and place their trades to take advantage it. For every "long" contract that a trader buys, anticipating higher oil prices, there must be a seller of the contract, anticipating lower prices. For some years, the price at which crude oil contracts change hands has tended to rise—albeit with some wide swings—and buyers often make money. They make money because the supply and demand situation has favored higher prices.

Polls indicate that when gas prices rise Mr. Obama's support among voters declines. Thus the need to scapegoat.

The reasons for higher oil prices (and a wide *general rise* in commodities prices such as oil, coal, copper, iron ore, gold, and many agricultural commodities) have been discussed at length. Chief among those causes are the surging economies of China and India, as their governments permit at least *relatively* freer markets, somewhat more secure property rights, and greater opportunity for private profit. Billions of individuals in these countries are more productive and able to demand (pay for) a higher standard of living. This explosive growth has made China, in just a couple decades, one of the world's largest consumers of oil, steel, coal, iron, copper, and a host of other commodities.

Pressures on the oil supply

Oil supply also has been affected, and uniquely, by geopolitics of the Middle East, Africa, and South America. Some of the world's largest oil producers are countries that have *reversed* the market process underway in China and India, damaging their economies and oil production. In one of the largest oil sellers to the United States, Venezuela, a socialist dictator has nationalized, looted, and crippled a once vibrant oil industry. The U.S. Energy Information Administration reported that "Venezuela's petroleum exports have dropped by almost 50 percent, since peaking at 3.06 million [barrels a day] in 1997." Socialist dictator Hugo Chavez was elected early in 1999.

President Obama shares a considerable amount of fair blame for the doubling of oil prices since he took office.

Iran, one of the largest oil exporters in the world, is a theocratic dictatorship, but, also, is hampered by worldwide economic sanctions. The International Energy Agency, the West's energy watchdog body in Paris, reported Iranian oil production fell to a 10-year low of 3.38 million barrels per day in February of this year. Recent oil industry reports suggest Iranian exports have fallen badly since then: from around 2.2 million bpd in February to 1.9 million bpd in March. The IEA emphasized that output could tumble to levels last seen during the 1980–88 Iran-Iraq war, when both sides' oil industries were strategic targets.

In the case of Iran, we also must wonder, from month to month, when and if Israel, with or without the active involvement of the United States, will launch a war that would devastate Iran's oil producing capacity and perhaps drive Iran to close off the flow of oil through the Persian Gulf.

Africa's major oil producer, Nigeria, is under attack from rebel forces that operate in its oil-producing region and regularly kidnap foreign oil workers.

I am not arguing here about policy toward Iran or about rebels in Nigeria. I am pointing out that there are valid and powerful causes for the rise in oil prices, and, in most cases, these problems are getting worse. For example, with daily talk and negotiations aimed at heading off war with Iran, isn't there reason for the price of oil to remain high?

Bring on those scapegoats!

Mr. Obama and his advisors are aware of all this. Indeed, it would not be implausible for Mr. Obama to point to these causes to explain why oil prices have *more than doubled* since he became president. Ah, but polls indicate that when gas prices rise Mr. Obama's support declines, and that prices at the pump threaten his re-election. Thus the need to scapegoat. Almost since organized economies have existed, the scapegoats for the consequences of government actions have been speculators, hoarders, and (in the Soviet Union and China) "capitalist wreckers"—and often the penalty has been death. Economists and historians have pointed out, routinely, that this is scapegoating—but apparently the temptation for politicians is overwhelming.

The political motivation behind Mr. Obama's attack on speculators was so obvious that the press felt free, even in news stories, to state it. Yahoo! News reported the story under the headline: "President Obama Targets Oil Speculators—Another Election Ploy?" *USA Today* wrote: "The plan is more likely to draw sharp election-year distinctions with Republicans than it is to have an immediate effect on prices at the pump." Stories almost uniformly commented that it wasn't at all clear that the measures would have any effect on gas prices.

But gas-pump pain is hurting Mr. Obama in the polls, threatening his re-election chances and Democrats in Congress urge him to attack because their re-election chances, too, are affected. That trumps all considerations of integrity in policy and truth in explanation.

Can speculators profit?

If economic reasoning were even a consideration in the President's proposals, he would have to deal with the demonstration by economists that speculators *cannot* profit from price increases that they themselves cause. If prices rise only because of buying by speculators, then, when speculators sell their positions, the sales will drive prices right down to where they were when the speculators began to buy. The first to sell might profit, but, as a group, the buyers will get the same average price at which they bought. They also will be out the costs of storing the commodity or keeping their investment funds tied up in the oil. Prof. George Reisman, in *Capitalism*, demonstrates this by diagramming the inevitable price movements and explaining the principles at work (pages 223–25).

A point made in news reports on Mr. Obama's speech is that studies show that activities of speculators do *not* increase the price of oil but *can* affect the shorter-term volatility—the ups and downs—of prices. Yet, according to

Mr. Obama, "investigations" have suggested, and at least one oil company executive has stated, that without speculation oil prices might be lower. This is completely *consistent* with the crucial role that speculators play in the market.

Speculators profit (if they do) by correctly anticipating future shortages of a product such as oil; their response is to bid up the price, which has the effect of limiting *present* demand (because higher prices reduce such demand). This, in turn, has the effect of reducing future shortages by limiting present consumption of oil. You may be interested in Prof. Reisman's brilliant exposition of this principle. Yes, speculators today, with good reason, foresee very real risks that oil supplies will plunge in the event of a war with Iran, for example; and so they bid up the present price of oil. This reduces demand now and so conserves oil for a time when it may be desperately needed.

But more is involved than the President, faced with blame for higher prices caused by worldwide supply and demand, trying to find scapegoats. And, of course, speculators—and Wall Street, in general—are excellent scapegoats at this time, since many millions of words have been written to try to blame them for the 2008 financial panic, stock market crash, and ensuing "Great Recession"—and to deflect blame from the government policies that made those catastrophes possible. Polls suggest that to blame Wall Street, investors and the wealthy is good politics at this time of economic fear and hardship.

The anti-oil President

The "more" that is involved, here, is that President Obama shares a considerable amount of *fair blame* for the doubling of oil prices since he took office. His rhetoric, decisions, and policies have discouraged, hampered, or choked off a greater supply of oil that would lead to lower prices. From the outset of his election campaign, four years ago, he has urged every possible alternative to oil— including solar energy, wind, and geothermal sources. He has campaigned for what he *sometimes* calls "independence from foreign oil"—but which is, in fact, independence from *oil itself*. (And he has slipped and said that several times.)

Just as consistently, his decisions have slowed or halted production of new oil. He cites statistics to counter the perception that he has been against oil production— claiming, for example, that there are more drill rigs today than when he came to office. But the issue is not whether there are more rigs but how many more *there could have been* and should have been in light of the unprecedented worldwide surge in demand for oil and potentially devastating threats such as loss of Venezuelan oil or a war with Iran.

Mr. Obama also says that oil production in 2011 reached an eight-year annual high. Other sources confirm this, but add that such production was *less* in 2011than in any years between 1950 and 1980. And Mr. Obama had nothing to do with the recent increase: Virtually all new drilling has taken place on *private* lands or state lands, where federal permission is not required to drill. In other words, companies gave up trying to get permission from the Obama administration to drill on federal land.

Mr. Obama has made so many decisions against oil production, and they are so complex (or deliberately obscured), that discussing them must await another article. Here are a few decisions that such an article would have to discuss.

During the administration of George W. Bush, when oil prices began to rise, President Bush reversed a policy instituted by his father, George W. H. Bush, and opened wide ranges of the Atlantic, Pacific, and Gulf coasts to off-shore oil drilling. When Mr. Obama came to office, he reversed that decision. Since then, his policy on off-shore drilling has been obscured by agreeing to such drilling and then qualifying it and endlessly delaying actual permissions—in one major case for a *five-year* environmental impact study.

The oil sands in Alberta Province, Canada, may contain as much oil as did the largest oil field ever known, in Saudi Arabia. To bring this oil to U.S. refineries, the Canadian government, against the usual environmentalist opposition, approved construction of a pipeline from the Canadian oil fields to the American Midwest and this was built. But the real need was to carry a much larger volume through a pipe that would run all the way to the great Texas oil refineries and ports. Again, in the face environmentalist and union protests, the Canadian government approved the "Keystone XL pipeline," which, so far, has been built to the Canadian border.

The XL pipeline was proposed in 2005. The usual almost endless environmental studies were completed and the company made more than 50 changes to the planned pipeline to reduce the chance of spills. Since then, the pipeline has awaited U.S. Presidential approval to cross the United States-Canadian border. Usually, this is a routine decision by U.S. agencies, but, faced with protests from environmental organizations, such as the National Resources Defense Council, President Obama stepped in and rejected the permit entirely.

The House of Representatives voted to speed up approval of Keystone XL. But polls showing that Americans, *especially* in the states affected by the pipeline, overwhelmingly support the project, has stiffened President Obama's spine to oppose the environmentalists in an election year. Thus, in March of this year, only three months after he withdrew the permission to build the pipeline, he gave a major speech in Cushing, Oklahoma—a huge oil hub—to announce he had "fast-tracked" the permission process. But that was for only part of the pipeline, and not the section from Canada. The rest of the project is on indefinite hold for additional environmental studies (and until after the election). To summarize Mr. Obama's on-again/off-again opposition, then support, for projects like this would require another article.

Mr. Obama, in his rhetoric of middle class versus rich, has proposed to raise more revenue by withdrawing "special privileges" and "subsidies" from oil companies. In principle, the government of a free market economy would not favor any industry by means of taxation or controls. But, within our complex, interventionist tax system, it is arbitrary to threaten withdrawal of tax benefits from oil companies—at a time we desperately need more investment in oil exploration.

What are these "special privileges" and "subsidies" that Mr. Obama would withdraw? He wants to reinstate royalty payments to the federal government from companies drilling in the Gulf of Mexico and end certain tax deductions for their development costs. In other words, government today is just not demanding *extra* payments for drilling the ocean bottom and is allowing companies to *deduct* certain business and development costs.

Speculating on the Obama effect

One of Mr. Obama's claims is true. He imposed regulations on automobile companies to require them to build more energy-efficient cars and trucks; another round of even tougher regulations is expected. This is one kind of "fix" the administration can manage: force businesses to spend more and, of course, consumers to pay much more, for cars that meet still higher fuel-efficiency requirements. There is no way to tell if the costs added to cars will ever be recouped by consumers through lower oil prices, especially since yet *another* round of regulations will dictate the size and weight of vehicles that companies can build. If only government could pass a law to make more oil appear in storage tanks! But dictates work only on people, not the laws of nature.

Those are several of a myriad of decisions, policies, and rhetorical attacks by which Mr. Obama has halted, slowed, discouraged (or played with substitutes for) production of more oil. His proposal to criminalize speculators, with no economic justification, cynically shifts the blame for political reasons. It will not bring down the prices at the pump. In fact, a speculator, whose role in the market, and personal goal, is to profit by *smoothing out* supply and demand between the present and the future, might well take Mr. Obama's proposals as an indication that oil prices will go higher.

After all, if re-elected, Mr. Obama may pop out of the closet as a full-blown radical environmentalist, opposed in principle to the exploitation of natural resources for human wealth. In any case, he would have four more years to subvert oil production in the name of "alternatives."

If passed by Congress, or implemented administratively, his crusade to criminalize speculation will undercut their crucial economic role: to minimize the impact of projected future shortages. If left alone, speculators would do this by bidding up the present price of oil, reducing demand now and conserving supply, thus lessening the impact of anticipated future shortages. Prices now would be higher, but prices later would be lower than they otherwise would be.

Mr. Obama is a bright man, surrounded by others of great ability and intelligence. The only plausible explanation for his proposals on speculation is dishonesty in pursuit of power.

Published *The Atlas Society*, April 25, 2012.

Health Care: The Road to Rationing
(August 2009)

A half-century ago, when the American medical care system was largely free and voluntary, and people regularly called it "the world's finest medical care," the advocates of the welfare state were able to converge on a strategy. They told people that they had a "right to health care."

Every argument and proposal for "national health insurance" (then called "socialized medicine" by its opponents, who had seen the complete takeover of medical care in Britain) included, as a basic premise, the merely asserted "right to health care." To all questioners the retort was "Would you let them die in the street?" Crudely but effectively, the moral premise was nailed into place, the only issue was implementation.

The "right to health care" sounded vaguely benevolent and caring. How can one ignore a sick neighbor? Of course, sick neighbors were not ignored. Doctors and hospitals routinely provided care, free of charge, to the indigent: not the most expensive care, but basic, sound treatment.

The "right" to end rights

In fact, however, the "right to health care" was revolutionary, in the precise sense of that word. It turned the concept of rights in the Declaration of Independence on its head. The rights to "life, liberty, and the pursuit of happiness [or property, in another formulation]" were rights to freedom of action—to live as one chooses, act as one wills, and keep the results of one's work. The "right to health care" had nothing to do with liberty or freedom of action. It implied that anyone and everyone was morally entitled to the services of doctors and nurses, the care provided by hospitals, the drugs developed and sold by drug companies, the services of a nursing home—all without concern for whose work made these possible, at what cost. The "right to health care" made irrelevant who would provide the services, who would pay.

How can one ignore a sick neighbor?

A "right" is not a right if honored only at the discretion of the provider; it cannot be the result of voluntary action. That would be a privilege. A right is a moral guarantee; in American parlance, rights are absolute and inalienable. If there are services to which people have a right, then someone has to be forced to deliver and pay for services; choice in doing so must be eliminated.

The philosophical hijacking of the concept of a "right" paid off in the political realm. In 1965, during the first administration of Lyndon B. Johnson, a protégé of FDR who sought to extend the New Deal with the Great Society, Congress passed and the President approved both Medicare and Medicaid, guaranteeing free medical and hospital care to all Americans over 65 years of age, whatever their income or wealth, and to Americans defined as below the "poverty level."

To get this legislation enacted past the opposition of the then-powerful organizations of physicians, such as the American Medical Association, Medicare simply offered to reimburse doctors and hospitals for the care they provided to elderly individuals: just send the bill and the government would pay it. For a few years, this provided a windfall for doctors and hospitals, who had been giving a great deal of charity care to elderly and indigent persons who could not pay. Or perhaps charging long-time patients, now elderly, less for services.

With all medical and hospital care now free to anyone over 65, or below the "poverty level," the cost of medical and hospital care to government rocketed past all estimates of the cost of Medicare. Initial cost estimates were exceeded by 100 percent, 200 percent, 1,000 percent, and today are projected, by sober actuaries, to portend the bankruptcy of America as the population over 65 keeps increasing. Yet, those over 65 now fiercely defend their "right" to free care, and, recently, in their name, organizations such as AARP demanded and received the addition of prescription drugs—said to be the single most expensive bill ever enacted in this country. At the same time, the demand unleashed on the medical and hospital care systems by Medicare and Medicaid helped to drive up the cost of medical and hospital care for everyone at a rate faster than almost any other category of good or service.

Morally intimidated by the cynically dishonest case of passersby leaving a dying man in the street, taxpayers were being saddled what became the single most budget-busting program of government. Only a crude appeal to altruist self-sacrifice could have covered up this gigantic bait-and-switch game.

After a few years, government realized that it must control the costs of medical and hospital care by rationing that care. No more just sending in the bill with "no interference in the practice of medicine." One of the earliest attempts was the system of Professional Standards Review Organizations (PSRO), through which government-created panels of doctors decided what medical and hospital care was and was not medically justified. Then came the craze for government-created or government-favored health maintenance organizations (HMO). Many, many other rationing schemes followed.

He who pays will control

Such rationing was part of the iron logic of the "right to health care." If there is a "right to health care," then government must be its upholder—as it upholds traditional natural rights to life, liberty, and property. Therefore, government must pay for the care. But a valuable good that is offered for free is demanded in unlimited quantities. Why should you do without any type of care—treatment, prevention, enhancement—if it is free? Given what the government is now paying for Medicare, and projections of population growth of those 65 and over, the government's financial obligation in future years exceeds any possible source of funds. Government must control costs by deciding who gets what care, when, and how much.

The stumbling block to government attempts at rationing care has been the continued existence of private insurance companies. Individuals know perfectly well, from their conversations with friends and relatives about that favorite topic, health and medical care, what is available. If certain services are provided by private health insurers, the government cannot get away with denying them, or rationing them (limiting them), for the large and politically powerful group of elderly persons on Medicare.

The only answer, politically, is to put all medical and hospital care under one payer—government. That is the thrust of the Obama administration's new bill to move toward the complete government takeover of health care. Of course, private insurers are not outlawed in the bill; instead, the government would become a major health insurer in competition with private companies. But with government providing insurance subsidized by taxes, borrowing, and the unlimited capacity to print money, who would win in this competition? Soon, there would be only one payer.

Republicans and some Democrats are now fighting this aspect of the bill, proposing, instead, some kind of nonprofit organization that would provide health care insurance to those unable to obtain it elsewhere.

But the underlying direction is clear, as it has been clear from the day that the advocates of the welfare state introduced the concept of a "right to health care." If everyone has a "right to health care" that only can mean a right to the state-of-the-art health care available at any given time. Because no government can afford to pay for everyone to receive the truly best medical and hospital care available, health care must be standardized, defined by government, and doled out in equal measure to all. This is the exact meaning of the proposal to tax companies that provide "Cadillac" health insurance to pay for the services that the bill would provide to those who cannot afford health insurance.

The "right" to rationed care

The "right to health care" will be achieved by rationing available care among all comers—those who can pay and those who can't—so all are equal. The equality will be achieved by averaging down—farther and farther down, as time passes. But in this way, the concept of a "right to health care" can be realized by the logic that everyone is getting the same care—at whatever level a debt-loaded, tax-gobbling, technically bankrupt government can afford. But first, the availability of private care must be ended.

Half a century after the battle cry "the right to health care" was introduced by the welfare statists, their bogus claim to the moral high ground has virtually overcome all principled opposition to socialized medicine. Only the details are now under discussion in Congress. With the passage of the Obama bill, serious rationing will begin, with the lines waiting for hospital and medical care, with the trips out of the country (but to where?) to obtain desperately needed care that have become everyday life in Britain, Canada, Sweden, and other havens of socialized medicine. There already are many systems, waiting in the wings, for determining what are the statistically highest-payoff diagnostic and treatment procedures—what will yield the average best results for the average patient. A high-priority consideration will be the average number of years of life a procedure will buy, which will make expensive treatments for older patients a bad bargain and a target for severe rationing.

Behold the long-term power of morality, the appeal to moral principle, in determining the course of a country's freedom or destruction of freedom. The only principled opposition to the "right to health care" in the 1960s came from Objectivists. The single best article refuting such a right appeared in the prestigious *New England Journal of Medici*ne. The author, Robert Sade, was a physician who was an admirer of <u>Ayn Rand</u>.

Without the irresistible long-term power of a rational moral code, the government takeover of medical and hospital care—complete, bureaucratic, and as innovative and compassionate as government bureaucracy—cannot be resisted. Today, the only arsenal with the firepower to prevail in the moral war for genuine rights and freedom is the philosophy of <u>Objectivism</u>.

Published on *The Atlas Society* August 10, 2009.

Freedom Is a "Crack"
(August 2009)

I am told that today's system of medical care in the United States lets too many people "fall through the cracks."

The phrase is one of many cliches that substitute for thought, or argument, in the debate over what, for short, is called "Obamacare," which is just another step in the long process of turning medical and hospital care in America into a completely nationalized industry.

The phrase has ranked for decades among the "Top Ten" sound bites about medical care because the phrase carries the whole load of hidden premises behind socialized medicine that are seldom openly identified. The phrase implies, for example, that medical care must be available to anyone at any time without regard for payment. If anyone goes without medical care at any point, then the system has a "crack."

But, since medical care requires the scientifically challenging and costly discovery and production of drugs and medical devices, the building and equipping of hospitals and other facilities of enormous sophistication, and the careers and devotion of highly trained professionals in dozens of categories—and since these resources do not exist in nature—where does this ideal system assumed by Crack Theory come from? What makes it the assumed objective of a medical care system to provide these services and facilities and drugs to every man, woman, and child at any time under any circumstances?

If no one must fall through a crack in the medical care system of the United States, then who must be forced to mortgage his or her plans, work, savings, and hopes to put in place and maintain this seamless system of services, facilities, drugs, and equipment to everyone—regardless of ability to pay, willingness to work, inclination to save, inclination to limit family size, inclination to smoke, drink, do drugs, or become obese?

A system of seamless servitude

And if, somehow, this seamless system of servitude, paid for and supplied by the productive to all comers, existing or yet unborn, must exist for medical care, then, by the same assumptions, it must exist for education, nutrition, housing, transportation...

All must be provided, 24/7, forever, to all comers in a seamless system in which no one will fall through any crack. Whatever the responsibility or irresponsibility of anyone for working, saving, having children they can afford, taking care of their health, *we still must be responsible* for creating and delivering all goods and services to them in a crack-less system.

Given such responsibilities, to be met through ever-increasing taxes, and debt to be paid or defaulted on by generations to come, there obviously would be *no crack* through which any of us could slip to have our own ambitions, our own long-range plans, our own income, our own savings—our own future that could be planned with our own efforts and resources.

There would be NO cracks—in a seamless system of lifelong obligations to provide all goods and services to all comers—through which we could slip to choose, plan, and live the course of our own lives. And that is the goal, and destination, and rapidly approaching reality of the system that is called "caring," "decent," and "humane" by the builders of socialism: *to leave no crack for individual freedom.*

Published on *The Atlas* Society on August 14, 2009.

Suing Apple for Keeping Products from Customers
(March 2012)

On March 8, 2012, the front page of the Wall *Street Journal* carried a weird story. It was weird because it involved what is arguably America's favorite company, Apple, and a significant action by the U.S. Justice Department—but there were no official sources. As far as one could tell, the story was based entirely on anonymous leaks and unofficial interviews. I didn't realize that our government could take action against a major corporation—in fact, six corporations—and keep it secret.

The story was that the U.S. Justice Department's Antitrust Division was "considering" a lawsuit against Apple and five major book publishers for "price fixing" and so making products less accessible to customers.

What products? Well, you have heard of the infamous so-called monopoly on oil, and on aluminum, and on electrical equipment, and on telephone services, and on computer operating systems—all legends in the history of antitrust prosecutions. Now, we have the infamous scheme to create an e-book trust and the new villain is Steve Jobs. Jobs is no longer available to prosecute, of course, but, based upon his supposed "price-fixing conspiracy," Apple is in trouble.

The allegation, as unofficially leaked to the *Wall Street Journal*, is that as Jobs prepared to launch the first iPad, he set out to price e-books in a new way. The established pattern in the physical book business is that the publisher sells the book to the retailer, who is free to set the retail price—presumably at a level that sells the most books at the highest profit. This is also how e-books were distributed at first. So, for example, Amazon was able to buy these books from publishers and set the retail price. In fact, Amazon at first may have used this discretion to sell e-books at a loss to encourage as many people as possible to buy a Kindle, its e-book reader.

Jobs supposedly told the book publishers that they should set the retail price of the e-book, which Apple then would sell and take a 30 percent cut. But he went on to stipulate that the book publishers should not permit any retailer to sell the same book for less than the set price. With the leverage of a deal reached with Apple, the book publishers were able to go to Amazon and get the same agreement. Hence "price fixing": an alleged conspiracy among companies to maintain a specific price for a product across the market. Under the antitrust laws this is known as a *per se* violation—illegal on the face of it, without considering intent or market impact.

Five major book publishers, Simon & Schuster, Hachette Book Group, Penguin group, Macmillan, and HarperCollins Publishers, Inc., are also being threatened with the Justice Department suit. Apparently, some or all of the companies have been negotiating for quite a while to reach a possible settlement—all in secret up until March 8.

Among the many problems with the antitrust laws, which have existed since the Sherman Act of 1890 and which include four subsequent major pieces of legislation, is that a businessmen never can be sure if he is violating them or not. It seems obvious that Steve Jobs did not realize that what he was doing was illegal because he carefully and fully described what he had done and why to his biographer, Walter Isaacson. Steve Jobs was not the kind of executive who gives interviews with his lawyer on his left and his public relations guy on his right. It seems apparent he made these comments because he did not consider that he might have been breaking the law.

A history of contradictions

This is not surprising. Throughout their history, the antitrust laws have been criticized as a mass of contradictions—undefinable in advance of suddenly hearing that you are being sued by the Justice Department. For example, Amazon, by selling e-books at a loss, may well have been charged with engaging in "predatory pricing" and "intent to monopolize"—sell at a loss to drive out competitors and then, as the only supplier in the market, charge monopoly prices.

The antitrust laws are an egregious example of non-objective law. Historically they have accomplished nothing.

There is not enough information (and no official information) about the Apple case upon which to base an analysis of the allegations, so my purpose here is only to point out that the whole history of antitrust has been one of mind-bogglingly complex and unpredictable litigation, the use of the antitrust laws by a business's rivals to gain an advantage, and what one Supreme Court Justice called "an element of sheer under-doggery"—the punishment of the most successful company in any given field.

Criticisms of antitrust existed from the start, but among the very first principled, consistent, and morally confident attacks on antitrust, and defense of its victims, was one by Ayn Rand. In the very first issue of *The Objectivist Newsletter*, in 1962, in a lead article entitled, "Choose Your Issues," Rand identified as the two greatest threats to capitalism, and therefore freedom, the antitrust laws and the Federal Communications Commission's (FCC) control of the airwaves. This and other seminal essays on antitrust by Rand, Alan Greenspan, and others can be found in the collection, *Capitalism: The Unknown Ideal.*

She made the economic point, which had been made before, that under *laissez-faire* capitalism it is impossible to sustain a non-coercive monopoly—a company or companies able to set prices without regard for competition. Both the logic of investment being attracted to fields where potential profits are highest and the historical record suggest that, without fail, competition in a genuinely free market is inconsistent with sustaining a monopoly.

With brilliant logic, she made the case she brilliantly and cogently made the case that all actual monopolies, which she termed "coercive monopolies"— such as some of the early American railroads—came into existence and were sustained only because they had the backing of government by means of subsidies, exclusive franchises, and special privileges. In case after case, the record shows that the infamous so-called "trusts" were either not coercive monopolies (for example, Alcoa Aluminum Company, which kept improving its efficiency and lowering its prices even without actual competition, and so kept the field unattractive to competitors) or were coercive because they enjoyed government backing (the notorious "Big Four" in railroads).

The values of free action, freedom of contract, and voluntary cooperation are systematically undercut by antitrust—in the name of "competition." But, most crucially, and perhaps for the first time, Rand made the moral case that decade after decade the major antitrust cases targeted the most successful, prosperous, and often largest company of the time—and tried to cut them down to size in the name of competition. In the late 1990s, the premier corporation in America in reputation and profitability was Microsoft and, true to form, it became the antitrust victim of the decade with an enormously expensive, complex court case over its alleged intent to restrict competition by using only its own Web browser.

Consistently victimizing the most successful

The Justice Department is nothing if not consistent in choosing its victims. Apple is among the most profitable, productive, and wealthiest companies in America. That is a sure signal to the minions of antitrust to bring it down.

The risks to a company of trying to defend itself from an antitrust suit have always been intimidating: the laws are contradictory, the definition of the crime is subjective, the choice of victims (from a legal standpoint) is arbitrary, and the Justice Department, liberal press, and the company's rivals join in convicting the company in advance in the court of the public opinion. And the Justice Department has unlimited taxpayer funds to spend, while the company bleeds year after year as the litigation drags on. In the 1970s, IBM was mired for 13 long years in an antitrust case brought by the Department of Justice. At one point, IBM had to retain more than 200 lawyers to conduct the case, including responding to the Justice Department's demand for millions of pages of documents. At the end, in 1982, the Justice Department dismissed the case as "without merit" and dropped it.

It was not surprising that one of the reported leaks to the *Wall Street Journal* from the book publishers quoted the source as saying, "a settlement is being considered for pragmatic reasons…" And "You have to consider a settlement whether you think it's fair or not." This is justice in the world of antitrust.

Also, of course, others have smelled blood in the water. There already are several class action suits against Apple, recently consolidated in a New York federal court. The incentive for private suits is nearly irresistible because under the antitrust laws a successful private suit can collect triple damages from Apple—a little spin included in the antitrust legislation to encourage private parties to join the attack on big, successful corporations.

Meanwhile, since 2010, when the first iPad was introduced and Jobs shaped the new pricing policy, sales of e-books have soared. In 2011 alone, sales more than doubled to $970 million.

What sustains the antitrust laws decade after decade? Plainly, they are an egregious example of non-objective law. And historically not only have they accomplished nothing, but have wasted a huge amout of taxpayer money and business resources and discouraged untold numbers of new ventures—ventures we will never know that were stillborn—by corporations afraid of stumbling into the ghastly circus called "antitrust."

One problem has been that for many decades conservatives supported the antitrust laws because they were defended in the name of competition, of keeping the economy "free." Behind this belief was both the misunderstanding of the early history of antitrust (the failure to distinguish between companies achieving success by productivity and companies entrenched by government action) and a *Through the Looking Glass* concept in economics called "perfect competition." You may wish to read about this concept in *Wikipedia*, but be warned that it makes the most abstruse legal document seem lucid. Suffice it to say this concept, which makes such assumptions as "perfect knowledge" and "perfect entry," is admitted by all concerned to have no application to the real world. What, then, is its supposed value?

Wikipedia explains that, though impossible, perfect competition is an "ideal" against which to measure real-world competition. Well, that is very convenient for those who would condemn competition, because, when measured by the standard of an impossible ideal, the real world will always fall short. (For a penetrating analysis of "pure and perfect competition" see *Capitalism* by Professor George Reisman, who explores the roots of the concept of perfect competition in a collectivist, or "tribalist," view of economics and demonstrates its use by contemporary economists to condemn capitalism *as such* not only alleged monopolies. See especially page 425 and following.)

The other crucial confusion is about competition. The antitrust legislation is based squarely on the idea that competition is an essential feature of a free economy, a primary value. But competition is not and cannot be primary because it is not a primary value; it is a consequence. The primary, in this case, is the individual's right to produce, trade, and, in doing so, use his property as he sees fit. As individuals strive to sell what they produce for the greatest profit, they will be in the market with other individuals trying to maximize their profits. The consequence will be competition, but the primary value is the freedom to act, to make contracts, to enter any voluntary arrangement. It is this freedom of the acting individual, this unrestrained application of reason to the problem of production, which creates the unique bounty and progress of *laissez-faire* capitalism.

It should be evident, at this point, that these values of free action, freedom of contract, and voluntary cooperation are systematically undercut by antitrust—in the name of "competition," which is in fact made possible only by the very values under attack.

And so, less than a year after his death, Steve Jobs, one of the giants of innovation and productivity of our time—a man whose genius and drive have brought untold hundreds of millions of people into the world of computing, communications, and unlimited access to information and entertainment—is being remembered by means of a prosecution justified in the name of defending consumers.

Published on *The Atlas Society* on March 9, 2012.

U.S. and Canadian Oil Drillers Frack the OPEC Cartel
(December 2014)

Gasoline is cheaper at the pump this week; my dental technician commented on it just today. And I am relieved that I can fill the Subaru Forester for under 50 bucks. Estimates are that, should current prices hold, the average American consumer will save $1,100 a year. Keynesians pray he will spend it, to 'stimulate' the economy; I hope he will save it to 'stimulate' the economy by increasing America's capital available for investment—the key determinant of both employment and pay levels.

Since June, the price of a barrel of oil has dropped some 40 percent from more than $100 a barrel to around $65. But relief at the pump and money to spend or save are the bread and circuses of the story; behind that cheerful façade, of course, are upheavals of world politics on a historic scale.

To put aside pretense: No one knows for sure why the price of the world's indispensable natural resource has plunged some 40 percent in six months. The only factor we know for sure, and can quantify, is that during that time the U.S. dollar, in which international oil is *priced*, has increased in value 10 percent, accounting for roughly a $10 drop in the $100-plus price of oil. The rest of the precipitous price decline has to do with demand (depressed economies consume less power), but also supply. Most commentators speculate that supply is the real story.

Nor can most OPEC oil producers survive long at a price of $60 a barrel: *not* because their costs are high but because they have built big welfare states on hyper-high oil revenues.

The OPEC cartel

Since World War I, but particularly during and in the aftermath of World War II, the Middle East became a dominant, and, then, obsessive, focus of the developed world—meaning Western Europe, the then Soviet Union, North America, Japan, and a few other nations. There certainly were other sources of oil: Texas, Oklahoma, Alaska, and the Gulf of Mexico in America; the North Sea oil fields off Scotland; Venezuela; and, when the Soviet Empire imploded, Russian oil fields. But no oil reserves were remotely comparable to those in the Middle East, especially Saudi Arabia, the United Arab Emirates, Kuwait, Iraq, and Iran. All other oil fields were being depleted; the Middle East oil reserves seemed inexhaustible.

And so the Arab nations, plus Iran, increasingly held the key to prosperity or calamity for developed economies. In the 1970s, in retaliation for support of Israel by the United States, Middle Eastern nations shut off oil entirely, helping to send America and Europe into depression and runaway inflation.

Although relations between the United States and the great oil producers, especially Saudi Arabia, have become regularized and cooperative, there have been—to say the least—irritations. For example, all 19 of the terrorists who brought about the 9/11 catastrophe were Saudis, as was their chief and mastermind, Osama bin Laden. Responding to 9/11, the United States invaded Afghanistan, and later Iraq. But nary a word was said against Saudi Arabia and the hyper-virulent brand of Islam its governing sheiks promote.

And that's how things seemed to remain, on the surface—indeed, with competition for Middle East oil becoming fiercer with gluttonous demand from the new economic prodigy, China. But things had started to change—slowly at first, and then, momentously.

The change was driven in large part by the sky-high price of oil maintained by the Organization of Petroleum Exporting Countries (OPEC), especially Saudi Arabia— despite the fact that it costs Saudi Arabia an estimated $2 to produce a barrel of oil it was selling for $100 or more.

New Technology = New Resources

Oil trapped in layers of sand and shale—huge pools of oil, matching Saudi Arabian reserves—were theoretically accessible in North America and Canada by using highly sophisticated new drilling technology such as horizontal drilling and the much-criticized 'fracking'. Oil sands and shale in Calgary, Canada; the Permian Basin in Texas and New Mexico; and the Bakken fields in North Dakota were awaiting oil prices that would make drilling profitable even by very expensive extraction methods.

Obligingly, world oil cartels such as OPEC, including many covert funders of radical Islam; adversaries of America such as Russia and Venezuela; and violent locals in Nigeria kept the price of oil as high as possible without quite cratering U.S. and European economies (their customers). But higher prices for oil meant that extracting those U.S. and Canadian oil deposits became realistic and profitable. By about a decade ago, American entrepreneurship was in full swing, with big investments from venture capital firms and support from investment in the stocks of the new companies.

And so we reach today's moment of truth.

Not Half Free: The Myth that America is Capitalist

As recently as June, the price of a barrel of oil hovered above $100. Iran, Saudi Arabia, Russia, and Venezuela all celebrated a vast transfer of wealth from the United States, Europe, Japan, and China to their own treasuries.

And then, the oil price started to fall–and has kept falling for five months in a row. Offered as an explanation is the depressed state of economies in the United States, Europe, and Japan—and reduced economic growth in China—and so less demand. Except that most of those economies had been far weaker after the 2008 financial crash and the United States, at least, has been recovering and growing again. And yet, only now is oil price plunging.

And so the other explanation. Not because of actions of the Obama administration, which has continued to limit drilling for oil off-shore and in Arctic waters, opposed a pipeline to bring Canadian oil to world markets, and resisted fracking, but as a result of extensive new high-tech drilling on non-federal lands, either private or state controlled. And because of the steady defiance by the new oil pioneers of opposition by environmentalists and regulators at every turn.

America is rapidly becoming a leading world oil producer on par with Saudi Arabia.

The vast oil reserves around Calgary, the Bakken, and the Permian Basin have come on line and, at least for now, are glutting the world with oil. After literally decades of talk about United States "energy independence" from Islamic Arab states, Russia, and the Venezuelan socialist dictatorship, America is rapidly becoming a leading world oil producer on par with Saudi Arabia.

Price War

And so we arrive at last week. Alarmed by the plunging price of oil—and of revenues that are virtually the only income of countries like Saudi Arabia, Russian, Venezuela, and Iran—OPEC met in Vienna to decide how to respond.

One choice: Reduce their own production, thus tightening supply, and hope that this would lift the international price of oil. Countries desperately dependent on oil prices for survival pleaded for this choice. It was not to be. The leading oil-producing nations like Saudi Arabia, with (very temporarily) huge financial reserves, adopted a longer-range strategy of price war. They gambled that by keeping the price of oil low, they could cripple, perhaps destroy, the new North American oil producers.

As mentioned, the long-established (mostly by Western companies) oil fields of the Middle East, with their infrastructure in place, can produce profitable oil at a few dollars per barrel. But the new, sophisticated technology of the North American oil producers requires a much higher "break even" price for oil. Roughly, overall estimates are that the North American producers can drill profitably at about $60–$70 a barrel. Oil today (December 5) closed at around $66 a barrel.

And so the lines of the battle are defined. If the oil price recovers from the current $66 a barrel, or at least falls no farther, domestic oil producers can drill and American energy independence just might become a reality. If so, we will be able, at last, to tell Saudi Arabia, Iraq, Iran, Russia, and Venezuela to 'get a life' apart from selling hyper-expensive oil to us. Iran will become far more dependent on integration into the world economy and even more vulnerable to economic sanctions. The great bankrolls behind the surge of Islamic radicalism will diminish. Russia may hesitate to finance armies in other countries, such as Ukraine. And China may start buying oil from America, reversing the flow of U.S.-Chinese trade and the balance of payments.

Today, no one can be sure what direction this price war will take. The new drilling technology is expected to get cheaper, over time, and more capital investment will mean more productivity. Nor can most OPEC oil producers survive long at a price of $60 a barrel: *not* because their costs are high but because they have built big welfare states on hyper-high oil revenues.

Nor is the United States—in theory—helpless to influence the outcome. For example, the Obama administration could ease environmental regulations and costs, enabling oil producers to lower their costs. The Obama administration could open arctic and off-shore waters to oil drilling, increasing the domestic supply at lower cost. It could drop its opposition to the Keystone pipeline and call its environmental dogs of war off the "fracking" chase.

Of course, it will do none of those things. The role of our government, it seems, is to appease environmentalists by regulating, controlling, and limiting production by the private companies.

Energy—and for historic reasons, oil—is the motor of the world. When there are seismic shifts in production and flow of energy, there are earthquakes in world politics. Earthquakes, for all our efforts, are unpredictable. But if the shift toward North American producers is real and enduring, then governments—and even nations—may rise or fall.

Published on "Financial Sense" on December 3, 2014 under the title "Pause at the Pump: Oil Politics Cause Earthquakes."

Competition Finally Upsets the Biggest Monopoly of All: OPEC
(December 2014)

"The U.S. will remain the world's biggest oil producer this year after overtaking Saudi Arabia and Russia in extraction of energy from shale rock spurs the nation's economic recovery, Bank of America Corp. said."

(Bloomberg News, July 4, 2014)

Without the coercive power of government (legal franchises, special privileges, favored treatment), no attempt at monopoly, a business able to sustain its prices without regard for competition, can prevail in free market. Its profits, above those prevailing in the market, will attract competitors, either producing its product or an alternative product, and they will gain market share by charging lower prices. The former monopoly will be forced to charge market prices or lose its customers. (The much-touted exceptions, beloved of anti-capitalist muckrakers like novelist Frank Norris, who wrote "The Octopus," are monopolies that enjoyed government backing, the most infamous examples being the transcontinental railroads backed by huge land grants, special port-entry privileges, and other favors. These are "coercive" monopolies.)

It is a logically beautiful theory, and unassailable, but for more than a century, since enactment of the Sherman Antitrust Act in 1890, inspired by fear of what, in fact, were coercive monopolies (railroads) or temporary dominance by a company in an infant industry (Standard Oil), U.S. law enforcement of "anti-trust" legislation has grown in scope and power. Among its great victims have been Standard Oil of New Jersey, Aluminum Company of America, General Electric, Microsoft, and Apple. The list runs into thousands, indicted or intimidated, and reads like a roll of honor of American capitalism.

How could this misguided, economically crippling, often bewilderingly arbitrary charade go on so long in defiance of logic? Because no demonstration in theory is proof against those who would exploit the complexities of economic life, as it actually exists, to challenge the theory—or, as in the case of antitrust law—excrete an ink cloud of confusion made possible by the welter of multiple causes of any phenomenon is a modern economy.

Now, we can get specific. Today, Americans, like most people in the world's industrialized economies, are experiencing a drastically drop in costs at the gas pump and when the oil-heating bill arrives. The chief cause represents a demonstration of the unsustainability of monopolies *even in a semi-free, all-too-regulated, semi-capitalist system.*

The demonstration takes the form of a plunge in the world price of a barrel of oil from more than $100 in September to about $55 as I write—a 40 percent price decline in one of the most important, pervasive commodities on the world market—literally, the engine of modern civilization. Headlines in the *Wall Street Journal*, the rest of the world financial press, but also the *New York Times* and every other news source, have trumpeted this astonishing crash in the oil price.

So much is widely known. Also known, to any reader of the press, is that the plunge in oil price results, at least in large part, from competition. After all, the dominant supplier of the world's oil for almost half a century has even had the name of a monopoly: the OPEC *cartel*. The Organization of Petroleum Exporting Countries was created 54 years ago by Arab nations led by Saudi Arabia (but including others, such as Venezuela and [later] Nigeria) to fix the world price of oil (previously, each oil company had set the price of the oil it produced, but OPEC members expropriated this power from the companies).

The OPEC cartel, in 1973, flexed its monopoly muscle by denying oil to the United States and Europe, and then greatly hiking its price, sending those economies into deep recession, in retaliation for support by Western nations of Israel's resistance to invading Arab armies. Back then, OPEC nations controlled two-thirds of the world oil markets. Oil drilling in Texas and Oklahoma, which once provided America with much of its petroleum, had peaked and was declining. OPEC called the shots and chose to do so as a cartel.

The economic response is a matter of record that I will not repeat here. The semi-free economies certainly did respond to the OPEC monopoly price. Out of Germany, Japan, South Korea, and Detroit came the first generation of very small, energy-efficient cars, and they kept getting better and more fuel efficient; energy-saving and energy-efficient homes became a new trend; and, by 1986, a barrel of oil that sold for $35 in 1980 was selling for $10. This is one way a free or semi-free economy responds to prices: demand for the product is reduced by many, often ingenious ways. And yet, in an economy only semi-free, such changes are never uncomplicated economic responses. During the 1970s, the United States was devastated by the imposition in 1973 of price controls, which made oil scarcities infinitely worse. The Reagan administration sought to trade advanced military hardware for lower Saudi oil prices.

The "supply" response

But what about the supply of energy? Who was competing with OPEC to share its monopoly profits? In the years after WWII, with the dramatic and terrible demonstration of the power of atomic energy, a trend arose in the 1950s toward the peaceful use of atomic energy and that trend kept growing until it seemed that every nation, every industry, and every power user—including especially the U.S Navy's submarine fleet—committed its future to nuclear energy. The excitement was enormous, with predictions of virtually free energy. Installed nuclear energy rose from less than one gigawatt in 1960 to 100 GW in the late 1970s to 300 GW in the late 1980s—an exponential growth of the kind that can revolutionize economies.

Certainly, government intervened, for example by setting a cap on the legal liability of nuclear power companies as the

The industry surged ahead on a wave of scientific and technological optimism, carrying the banner "peaceful use of the atom," but with too little attention to education of the American public who were their customers. And their neighbors, since nuclear power plants had to be constructed *somewhere*, in someone's "backyard." Seldom has the importance of the intellectual—the thinker, writer, editorialist, newscaster, or public advocate—in interpreting the world to the public been demonstrated more decisively than in the fate of the U.S. nuclear power industry. In this case, the demonstration decidedly was in the negative. What happens when intellectuals, for philosophical reasons, turn against science, technology, and economic progress *per se*? That is the story of the environmental movement as it became taken over by leaders who viewed man himself, his survival by productive use of his environment, as a blight on the "natural order."

Irrational fears of nuclear power overwhelmed the record in reality of the nuclear power industry. But this could not have happened without the active involvement of the intellectuals whose job it was to bring reason and science to the public debate. Instead, they whipped up the fears of the public on every occasion, ignoring the actual record of the nuclear power industry and embellishing on the fantasies and fears of the public.

This rising environmental/ecology movement exploited to the utmost the fears and ignorance of the public about the process that produces nuclear weapons— fears all-too-real in the Cold War nuclear confrontation between the Soviet Union and the free world—to attack the nuclear power industry. The indictment was not a "true bill." The undifferentiated packaging of the horrors of nuclear explosions with the risks presented by nuclear power plants was dishonest. Responsible scientists continually pointed out the misstatements, fallacies, and outright lies.

Of course, the nuclear power industry did not *arise* in response to the OPEC cartel; it preceded it. Scientific and technological advances driven forward by exigencies of war always have led to technological progress when peace arrives—at least in free markets ever alert to new sources of profit. But nuclear power became exactly the kind of "in waiting" technology that ambushes any attempt at monopoly; given monopoly prices, the latent—in this case, experimental—technology takes off. And the nuclear power industry both took off—and crashed—during the 1970s.

Nuclear power entered its commercial phase in the 1970s. Between around 1970 and 1990, more than 50 gigawatts (GW) of capacity was under construction, but the *peak*, at more than 150 GW, was in the late 70s and early 80s. Environmentalist attacks had dogged the industry almost from the start. But environmentalism, like nuclear power, was new. When it began to focus on litigation as a way to *delay* construction of nuclear power plants at every phase—delays that cost the industry hundreds of billions of dollars (*e.g.*, in interest on financing and delay of income)—environmentalism won. The massive upfront expense of constructing safe nuclear power plants, the huge financing required, the litigation invited by 'public responsiveness' of federal regulatory agencies, the possibilities of litigation at several levels, at every stage, proved to be the giant killer.

But the nuclear power industry pushed ahead, doing much better in some locales (the South, the West) than in other places (New York, New England, and California) where trends such as environmentalism were embraced by a liberal-left establishment and press. The blow that checked the momentum of the industry, and from which it never has recovered, was the accident in 1979 at Three Mile Island. Coverage by the media created a harrowing story, and, indeed, the accident was serious, with evacuations and disruptions of residents and lingering fears of contamination. A startling fact was evident immediately: There were no casualties. Not one. But the press highlighted the risk of longer-term effects of radiation; the population displaced by the accident returned home in terror of radiation exposure. We know, now, that every study and assessment of the effect on the population has revealed *no* increased health problems—after more than 30 years of intensive monitoring.

The supply response: "cancelled"

It didn't matter. Nuclear power to generate energy in the United States, and to compete with the OPEC cartel (then already 13 years old), lost its momentum, and, to this day, has not recovered it. More than two-thirds of all nuclear plants ordered after January 1970 were eventually cancelled. In particular, though, a total of 63 nuclear units were canceled in the United States between 1975 and 1980—after Three Mile Harbor cancellation became an avalanche.

This was not the end of nuclear power. Nuclear power in the United States, today, produces 19 percent of our electricity. It is the most nuclear energy produced in the world; but, relative to population, for example, nuclear power produces 80 percent of electricity in France. And nuclear power plants proliferated, for example, in Japan, Israel, and few other nations without powerful environmental movements, more generally educated publics, and more informed about science. All this occurred decades before the Fukushima disaster in Japan, probably a once-in-a-century series of improbable events, one with wide and devastating costs. And yet, the World Health Organization reports that evacuees were exposed to so little radiation that radiation-induced health impacts are likely to be below detectable levels. No deaths were reported as resulting from the accident.

But for our story, here, of how free markets can respond with new supply to prices that monopolies and cartels seek to impose, nuclear power became irrelevant. Plants already existing produce power (and in the United States, no notable accident has occurred since 1979; deaths caused by nuclear power plants in America remain at zero—making it widely recognized as the safest major source of power in our history). But the growth of nuclear power became *irrelevant* as a supply response to the OPEC cartel—and the trillions of dollars in national wealth transferred from America to Saudi Arabia and the other great Arab nations.

Nuclear power had been a sweeping, innovative response of the market to OPEC's monopoly prices, a response playing to America's strengths in science and technology. And it was a revolutionary response. Carbon-based fuels would be left behind: the coal-fired plants, the gasoline-powered internal combustion engines, the oil furnaces, the oil-powered utilities—all would be superseded by a potentially unlimited supply of nuclear power, producing almost none of pollution associated with carbon-based fuels. And if nuclear fission, the process that produced the atomic bomb, were supplanted by nuclear fusion, the source of power of the sun, then, yes—an era of unimaginable abundance of energy, at virtually no cost, would be upon us.

This is how capitalism—the freedom of innovators and producers to profit by creating new technologies, by making obsolete what once was indispensable, ushering us into the future—works. But reality, while it does not negate a true theory, may greatly complicate its impact.

The monopoly triumphant

For three long decades, from 1980 to 2010, the OPEC cartel dominated the world oil market. The great sheikh families of Saudi Arabia played their hand craftily; their partnership with the U.S. government became exceedingly close. The U.S. Energy Information Administration estimated (as of 2009) that it costs Middle East producers less than $10 a barrel to "lift" their oil: maintain and operate the wells and related facilities and equipment; and less than $7.0 a barrel to find new resources—except that there often is little need for new resources. All the technology is Western as are all the great oil companies that keep the oil flowing. For the most part, that technology has become old-fashioned; but it has not mattered; drilling into the vast reserves beneath the desert is uncomplicated.

The sheikh families of Saudi Arabia, by far the largest producer, extend into the hundreds and most are billionaires. Their yachts are seen in the all the swank harbors of Europe, especially Monte Carlo; their consumption of the services of the most elite French prostitutes is a matter of record. A massive transfer of wealth from the "consuming" nations to the "producing" nations has gone on for decades. With the emergence of India, the People's Republic of China, South Korea, Vietnam, and other nations into the industrial, modern economy, the demand for oil has become fiercely competitive.

New oil supplies from the North Sea ("Brent"), Nigeria, Finland, and the Artic, including even the United States, provided some competitive supply of oil to check OPEC. And the canny sheikhs of Saudi Arabia were aware of that raising oil prices too high could push their Western customers into recession, lowering demand for oil. And this cozy relationship benefited the sheikhs; no word from Western governments criticized the adamantly authoritarian, undemocratic, primitive rule of the Sheikhs. The murderous attack of September 11, 2001, an attack on civilization itself in the form of the World Trade Towers in downtown New York City—killing thousands of Americans and hundreds of nationals of other countries— was carried out by 19 Saudi Arabian nationals and planned and directed by a Saudi Arabian national, Osama bin Laden. The U.S. government responded with not one word of criticism of the Saudi Arabian sheikhs, who promote a virulent fundamentalist version of Islamic religion.

In short, the OPEC cartel looked exactly like a government-protected monopoly, cozy with governments, resting on inside "understandings"—and draining trillions from U.S., European, and Asian economies in monopolistic profits that financed huge welfare states in the Arabian OPEC nations to pacify their populations—and leaving, in Saudi Arabia, two-thirds of the profits to the ruling families.

A semi-free, over-regulated Market—but still a market

Given the theory of the destruction, by free markets, of any attempted monopoly pricing, it may seem discomfiting that it took more than three decades for the market to respond decisively to the OPEC cartel (and the story is far from over as we shall see).

We have discussed how the supply challenge from nuclear power became permanently hobbled. In addition, as is well known, requiring little elaboration here: Every initiative of the U.S. oil-drilling, refining, and shipping industries ran into opposition, regulatory delays, and political stonewalling by government. Whether it was opposition to off-shore drilling, to drilling in the Alaskan wilderness, or building a pipeline to bring Canadian oil to U.S. refineries, it ran into regulatory hurdles, litigation by environmentalists, or became a political football. The sheikhs of the Middle East had staunch allies among the U.S. environmentalists and in the U.S. government. This has cost Americans, Europeans, and Asians many decades of paying monopoly prices for gasoline, heating oil, the firing of utilities, and the price of all transportation and almost all that they buy.

Despite all of it, and coming forward now to the present, U.S. and Canadian economies, and their innovators and entrepreneurs, against the opposition of regulators and sundry environmentalists, have asserted their classic role: disruption of settled, cozy markets—in bed with governments—to send earthquakes beneath the comfortable monopolies.

American industry already had exploited the readily accessible oil reserves of Texas and Oklahoma. Other oil resources—huge resources—lay beneath the ground in Texas, Oklahoma, the Dakotas, and much of western Canada—but were inaccessible to present technology or too expensive to drill. Thus, as the technology evolved in sites from the North Sea to the Gulf of Mexico to Venezuelan waters advanced—and as the OPEC oil prices reached $100 a barrel—the North American oil drilling industry slowly, then not so slowly, came alive.

In truth, it never had died. It had kept drilling, experimenting, testing new methods, seeking fields more accessible. But then, perhaps 10 years ago, the oil price (and so potential profits), the technology, and the availability of capital (in the form, often, of less-than-investment-grade bonds or "junk") came together to light a fire under the North American petroleum industry.

One technological key was horizontal drilling, which could follow the snaking flow of oil deposits between shale layers; another was the ability to get at and use the heavy petroleum from the vast oil sands of Canada; and, as we all know, hydraulic fracturing, or "fracking"—the injection of fluids under super pressure to crack layers of shale to get the oil and natural gas flowing. In Texas, the Bakken of North Dakota, and the vast oil sands of Alberta the new oil pioneers were drilling, accessing the elusive deposits, and increasing the efficiency of drilling. There was opposition at every step from environmentalists and regulators sympathetic to them. "Fracking," an innovation that made the vast reserves of oil in layers of shale available, was made a scare word by environmentalists.

But the North American entrepreneurs persisted, lured by monopoly prices sustained by the OPEC cartel, which made even difficult-to-access oil profitable. The impact on the market was long in coming, as the North American drillers grew, but what they had accomplished burst on the scene in September of this year. The price of oil in little more than four months plunged from $100 a barrel to $55 a barrel as of this writing.

In truth, several powerful factors came together to make the plunge in the price of oil so precipitous. One such cause was a sharp rise in the international exchange value of the U.S. dollar. For historical reasons, all oil worldwide is priced in dollars and the dollar has gained some 10 percent against the value of major world currencies. This automatically yields lower dollar prices for oil, but accounts for less than one third of the plunging oil price.

Another cause of plunging prices may be slackening demand—a favorite explanation in the financial press. After all, the world still is recovering from the once-in-a-century financial crisis of 2008, and the market crash and economic recession that ensued. The huge U.S. economy has been in recovery, with industrial production increasing, but European economies are still struggling and the long Chinese economic boom is cooling. The net impact on oil demand? Arguably demand is greater today than any year since 2008 given the recovery of the American economy; however, falling demand alone cannot explain the recent crash in the oil price.

A July 4 celebration

What is indisputable is that production of oil in North America in 2014, for the first time in *decades*, has caught up with Saudi Arabian production. *Bloomberg News*, on July 4, in a kind of unintentional celebration of American independence, wrote:

"U.S. production of crude oil, along with liquids separated from natural gas, surpassed all other countries this year with daily output exceeding 11 million barrels in the first quarter…The country became the world's largest natural gas producer in 2010. The International Energy

Agency said in June that the U.S. was the biggest producer of oil and natural gas liquids."

It is a true revolution in production. OPEC has taken note, to put it mildly. Meeting in Vienna this month, OPEC members debated what to do about the crashing world oil price. The world's media were there to watch every moment. World stock markets held their breath.

Many rulers of OPEC nations have kept their grip on power by means of distributing oil revenues; they pleaded for a decrease in OPEC production of oil, which would "stabilize" prices. The boss of the cartel, Saudi Arabia, staked out a more strategic position, worthy of a serious monopoly, ready to do battle for its position: keep oil production steady. (Saudi Arabia, almost alone among OPEC nations, has the financial reserves required to conduct a long price war to cripple their North American competitors while still funding their welfare state.) Saudi Arabia is calculating that a plunging world oil price will destroy the new North American drillers, who require higher prices. Their technology is decades ahead of Saudi Arabia's but makes it more expensive to drill.

The world financial press is buzzing with speculation about the outcome of this price war. The new North American drillers, as start-up enterprises, and growing at top speed, are heavily in debt. *Bloomberg News*, in the same story, pointed out that "Annual investment in oil and gas in the country is at a record $200 billion, reaching 20 percent of the country's total private fixed-structure spending for the first time."

Can the North American drillers continue their operations, and remain solvent, at a world oil price that has plunged from by almost 50 percent? If the price remains suppressed below $60 a barrel, consumers will pay less for gas, heating oil, utilities, and anything that involves transportation, but can the North American oil producers survive?

It is a classic 'price war' in which the reigning monopoly, or cartel, drives down prices, taking temporary heavy losses, to destroy competitors. OPEC is acting like a classic monopoly. Doesn't the classic view of monopolies imply that such tactics must fail? That the non-coercive monopoly, or cartel, cannot persist?

That is the theory in the context of a genuinely *laissez faire* economy, If the North American competitors operated in such an economy, they would not face (in the United States) the highest corporate tax rates in the developed world. They would not face costs of complying with regulation driven by environmentalists in and out of government. They would not face literally years of delay, by politicians such as Barack Obama, politically beholden to environmentalists, in a crucial project such as the Keystone pipeline. They would be fully free to compete.

To take just one example: How free are the North American oil companies to seek the profits they need to survive? Consider his final quotation from *Bloomberg News*: "A U.S. Commerce Department decision to allow the overseas shipment of processed ultra-light oil called condensate has fanned speculation the nation may ease its *four-decade ban* on most crude exports." [Emphasis added] One of the most dramatic demonstrations, in our day, of the theory that free competition makes non-coercive monopolies unsustainable, hangs in the balance. The theory is not in doubt, but the outcome of the demonstration is. Even one of the "freest" economies, the United States, is heavily compromised by regulations and oppressive taxation. And economies never operate independently of the level of understanding of their populations (look at nuclear power). And, finally, freedom depends upon the leadership of intellectuals whose sacred responsibility is to combat, not exploit, the ignorance and fears of the public.

Published on *Financial Sense* on December 16, 2014.

A New Way to Fix the Debt Crisis: Unchain Atlas

America's skyrocketing national debt forces us to make hard choices. Do we go bankrupt? Raise taxes? Make (politically impossible) entitlement cuts? Perhaps, instead, we should simply cut wasteful and costly government regulations.

The federal budget deficit for December came in at around $80 billion. This was the 27th month in a row that our government ran a budget deficit. As it regularly does, year after year, Congress is now considering raising the "debt ceiling"—the total debt the federal government is permitted to assume.

A poll today, however, reports that 70 percent of Americans oppose raising the debt ceiling, only 18 percent approve raising it, and 12 percent are perhaps honest enough to say they don't know. But Timothy Geithner, the U.S. Secretary of the Treasury, said this week that failure to raise the debt ceiling would lead to "catastrophic consequences"—that is, the federal government might default on paying existing debt; the government can only meet payments on existing debt by taking on more debt.

Can we really expect to cut spending?

Republicans reportedly are gearing up to oppose raising the debt ceiling unless the Obama administration agrees to reduce long-term spending. The problem is that other recent polls leave no doubt at all that most Americans strongly oppose cutting the spending that is really breaking the budget.

Virtually every economist points to so-called "entitlements" and, overwhelmingly, to Medicare, as the budget buster and the not-so-long-term fiscal Armageddon. Only about 20 percent of those polled would want to see Medicare cut. Nor would they cut federal spending on education.

About half of Americans would countenance cuts in military spending, and in my opinion that should be done—certainly on the strategic side, where our naval and air power utterly dwarf those of any other country or group of countries and have no reasonable, foreseeable mission in the world. But the lion's share of spending today is on the wars in Afghanistan and Iraq, where we spend $1 billion a day, monotonously, day after day.

But, while reductions of military spending would help, it would not solve the budget crisis, especially not in the long-term, because more than half of spending is built in, by law, to provide Medicare, Medicaid, and Social Security—which latter is paid entirely out of current funds, as there is nowhere that anyone's payments are invested and waiting to support them—to everyone who qualifies.

Can we afford to raise taxes?

Besides reducing spending, especially on benefits like Medicare, there is increasing taxation—the other side of the equation that is always is mentioned. There may come a time, and soon, when this must be done. The State of Illinois recently voted a huge increase in income and corporate taxes, and the governor will sign the bill. Apparently, it is that or default on debt—exactly the dilemma that faces the federal government.

One problem with raising taxes is that every single tax increase in history has been spent, in its entirety, by the government, but has never made possible a balanced budget for long, and *never* any significant paying down of accumulated debt. Instead, spending has outrun taxing, incurring deficits and increasing the total national debt and the now-staggering interest payments on it.

Theoretically, it is possible to increase taxes enough to pay for all spending and even to begin to reduce the national debt. Such taxes would fall on a relatively small percentage of the population because about half of all Americans pay no federal income tax at all—though a larger percent contribute payroll taxes for Social Security and Medicare.

For many decades, now, the economic growth of the United States has been slowing down. There is far less investment in the economy by Americans; we have depended very heavily on investment by foreigners, who have been buying up American companies and American assets. Also, there is a long-term migration out of the country by companies, especially in manufacturing, to reduce their overall costs, including taxes, wages, and the regulatory burden.

The people and companies on whom very heavy new taxation would fall are the ones who still have the surplus income to invest. In particular, there can be no increase in taxation on the half of Americans who pay federal taxes without taxing small businesses, because many of them are owned by individuals and families and their earnings and profits are income to those families.

As most people know by now, some 80 percent of new jobs are provided by small businesses. But the decade from 2000 to 2010 was the first decade since WWII in which the United States added *no* new jobs; the net job increase was zero. In the current recession, it is small businesses that have experienced virtually no recovery—

unlike large corporations that are able to find markets abroad.

The reason unemployment is so high, and so resistant to improvement, is that small business has to rely on selling to the domestic market and Americans are "de-leveraging" their balance sheets—reducing debt—after a decades-long credit expansion that ended in the financial crash and recession.

So here it is: Spending and debt are out of control. We don't want to increase borrowing. We don't want to impose taxes that would strangle any chance at creating new jobs. We don't want to cut the benefits that are really busting the budget.

So we face an oncoming debt tsunami and are helpless, politically, to save ourselves?

A third way: unchain Atlas by cutting regulations

There is another way, and it is readily suggested and documented at the site of the Americans for Tax Reform's Center for Fiscal Accountability.

All you need to know is there, on one page, and it boils down to the value of *massive de-regulation.*

This is what you will read at the site:

1. Each and every year, compliance with government regulations (time, professional services, and equipment) consumes about 17.7 percent of U.S. national income. If we translate that into the life of average working American, it means that Americans work 61 days each year for the income they spend on complying with regulation— either personally, or, to a much great extent, the additional amount they pay for goods and services because in the price is included the company's or other provider's costs of complying with regulations.

2. That cost of compliance does not include the economic impact of regulation in terms of limiting

production or distorting economic choices. As the Center for Fiscal Accountability puts it: "These hidden costs stifle the growth of the economy because they introduce inefficiencies and distortions and reduce the economic reward left over for productive activity." The best available estimate of that regulatory damage to the economy is $1 trillion a year.

3. Apart from these costs is the cost to government of enforcing the regulations, a cost that has gone up year after year as regulation has increased. The annual cost to government now is about $61 billion a year.

Here is the money we need to avoid debt catastrophe. The logic is quite simple: Don't begin by slashing benefits. Don't begin by instituting major new taxation. Begin by freeing up the economy, the American economic engine, to produce more wealth. For those of us familiar with the works of Ayn Rand: "Unchain Atlas."

The wealth produced by an economy freed from the huge burden of regulation could be taxed at the same level as today but yield much, much more revenue. The cost of complying with regulation would become freed-up income to Americans to spend and so give a huge boost to small businesses. And the government budget itself could be reduced by closing the regulatory agencies and putting their talented staffs to work in the economy—producing, not hampering production.

What regulations could be cut?

You can read about the economic burden of compliance, in brief or at length, at the site to which I refer. The Environmental Protection Agency and Homeland Security are big offenders; but a moment's consideration brings to mind regulation in every area of life.

The Sarbanes-Oxley Act drives companies to list their stocks abroad, and the effects of the huge financial regulation package passed by the Obama administration are too new to estimate accurately. But all anti-trust laws, relics of the nineteenth century, are unnecessary and protect no one except less able competitors. Environmental laws consume gigantic amounts of capital every year, even though United States air quality and the water supply are hugely cleaner and better than they were 20 years ago.

Give it all a rest, a complete rest, for 10 years. Occupational Health and Safety regulations could be left to the trial lawyers, who already exact a staggering toll from hospitals and businesses. One idea is just to put regulations on hold for a full decade, creating a holiday from regulations and regulatory compliance.

We may lose some benefits of regulation, yes. But something has to give, and soon. We face a national emergency, a situation that has been building for decades and is hurtling toward crisis. We face huge unemployment. We are losing manufacturing abroad.

Let Republicans pose this to the American people: We can slash Medicare, education, national parks. Or we can impose new taxes at a time when business has produced no jobs, net, for a decade and unemployment is stubbornly at 9.5 percent (official) and 15-20 percent (unofficial reality).

Or we can drastically deregulate the U.S economy, on a trial basis, for ten years to free up American productive power, give everyone more income immediately, and provide a huge boost to small businesses—on which the chief regulatory burden falls—who could begin to grow and hire again.

That's the choice. It seems to me when the choice comes down to lose benefits, get taxed, or face your fears that somehow suspending regulations—most of which did not exist 20 years ago, or even 10 years ago—will bring about some undefined disaster—that deregulation might win the "least ugly" contest.

The Republicans could write an omnibus deregulation bill and spell out exactly what could be saved, what economic growth would do for tax revenues, and how deregulation would get the American jobs engine running after a decade-long stall.

I think the Tea Party might be able to sell this. What do you think?

_____

Published on the *Atlasphere.org*

Sharia Zoning
(August 2014)

My town's zoning board, the East Hampton Village Zoning Board of Appeals, met last week and heard several appeals. Two of them made headlines in the *East Hampton Star*— one involving Steven Spielberg of movie fame, the other Dylan's Candy Bar. No doubt, "Steven Spielberg" catches your eye, and I will get to that, but, for my purposes, the Dylan's Candy Bar decision is more illuminating.

Dylan's Candy Bar, on Main Street, would like to serve hand-scooped ice cream—ice cream in cones—but this required a variance in zoning law. It was considered a 'nonconforming use' and there were concerns about litter outside on the sidewalk. Sticky ice cream spatters.

Dylan's resorted to a time-honored tactic in politics. It hired an attorney with clout and connections. Handling the appeal was Andrew Goldstein, former chairman of…the Zoning Board. He argued that a prior tenant of the same store, Nuts about Chocolate, represented a 'legal, pre-existing nonconforming use' and operated till 2006.

The Town of East Hampton Zoning Law (or 'Code') has a section on 'nonconforming' use, mostly addressing 'grandfathering' certain uses that predated the latest version of the code. More relevant, here, are the overall purposes of the Code and the mission of the Board of Appeals. One such purpose is "orderly growth… beneficial to the interests of the people"; another is "protection of…the value of private and public property"; another is "proper use of land: to promote, in the public interest, the utilization of land for the purposes for which it is the most appropriate..." and so on. The final item on this list is worth quoting in full; it captures the spirit of the Code as a whole:

"Aesthetic attributes: to perpetuate and enhance areas of natural beauty, to retain outstanding water views and other open vistas available to residents and visitors and to perpetuate generally those aesthetic attributes and amenities which not only please the eye, but which together are the essence of the nationally recognized character of the Town."

You can see that the five good burghers sitting in judgment of the appeal of Dylan's Candy Bar had some leeway. In fact, based on the wording the Code, with criteria such as "the public interest," purposes...most appropriate," "please the eye," and "the essence of the nationally recognized character of the Town" they could rule ANYTHING.

But, of course, they couldn't. Because it is "understood" by all that the point of zoning is to do the correct thing, the aesthetic thing, the thing consonant with our town's "recognized character." And these, at any given time, are expressions of the preferences, tastes, sense of style, and vision of the good of the Ladies Village Improvement Society, influential businessmen, real estate brokers, environmental and conservation groups, civic beautification organizations, editorialists of the *East Hampton Star* and *Dan's Papers*, and the collective exertions of lawyers retained to work the system for clients who can afford it.

How did we live without zoning?

It may surprise some that the practice of zoning didn't begin at all until New York City initiated it around 1920. Until then, our great cities and thousands of towns and villages survived essentially without "land planning" for private property. People endured neighborhoods with houses of different sizes, buildings of different heights, stores beside homes, big lots next to small lots, and no one to safeguard the "character" of the town or views "pleasing to the eye." How could so many millions fall in love with the vitality, excitement, and charm of their cities and write with such poetic passion about their towns and villages?

Zoning and related practices are called "law." There are fines and prison sentences to enforce the decisions of the Appeals board. But it is not law as most of us think of the law: a statement of what is permitted and what is not permitted in a way that can be known in advance, be the basis for objective rulings, and be understandable without legal counsel.

No, it is subjective and arbitrary: subject to interpretation by those with finer tastes and perceptions, those who can speak for "the public interest," those who have understood and can be guardians of our town's "character." It is more like Islamic Sharia law: the codification of the moral sensibilities, perceptions of propriety, and vision of the good of the "community," or "public," as represented by the taste makers. How women should dress, how much of the body it is appropriate to reveal, what social relations are permitted, what language is permitted, what entertainment and information permitted— all subject to interpretation from village to village, time to time, enforcer to enforcer.

Except that ours is Sharia law directed at private property, which, I guess, we view as a matter for collective, if ever-changing, standards. But what about property rights—the right to use and disposal of what we own? How does zoning square with that?

In a word: it doesn't. It does not have to. The law of the land is set forth in the *U.S. Constitution* and the Bill of Rights does not include one to protect property. But the

Constitution does include the Tenth Amendment, which reserves to the states, and to the people, all powers not granted to the federal government in the *Constitution.*

We are talking here about who wields the "police power." The powers not granted the federal government in the *Constitution* are reserved to the states. In most case, the states have chosen to leave matters of zoning to the police power of local governments. At the local level, there is essentially only one firm protection of property rights guaranteed by the *Constitution.*

The Fifth Amendment to the *Constitution* states that we cannot be deprived of our property without due process. When government takes our property (a "taking") by eminent domain, we must receive "just compensation." That, in effect, is the other face of zoning—"real law," as it were.

Dylan's Candy Bar and Spielberg's Horse Bath

Return now to Dylan's Candy Bar, standing before the Zoning Appeals Board, seeking a ruling that it may serve scooped ice cream. The board ruled, "yes," go ahead and scoop, because, although it is a "nonconforming use," there is a precedent.

That's all? We can leave? Go back to our store and start scooping?

Not quite. There is still the "public interest," "aesthetic," and "recognized character." You have your permit, but 1) you must power wash the sidewalk outside your shop at least once a day; 2) you must install and regularly empty outdoor garbage receptacles; 3) your ice cream sales are restricted to a specific area of the store; and 4) you cannot construe this permit to allow any other type of over-the-counter sales.

Other than the need to obtain the permission of the Suffolk County Department of Health Services to serve ice cream, that seemed to represent the considered voice of the East Hampton collectivity, at least that evening.

I promised to reveal the fate of Mr. Spielberg's appeal. The board ruled that his 5.5-acre property was sufficiently large, and shielded by a fence, tall hedges, and mature trees, so that a garage and storage facility, horse-washing facility, and tree house—all within the required 80-foot front yard setback from the road—did not affect his neighbors or "the character of the neighborhood."

You might wonder about that horse-washing facility as it relates to the "character of the neighborhood," but it seems that all facilities were there when Mr. Spielberg bought the place, so perhaps the neighborhood had adjusted to them. I'm sure the members of the Zoning Board could explain it to you.

What other threats to the public interest, aesthetics, and character of our town were addressed in the same week? Just to stick with those reported in the *Star*:

Sag Harbor village officials hit page one by "mulling" a 180-day moratorium on approval of "wetlands variances" for builders. It seems that homeowners are building too fast and ig, so that Mayor Brian Gilbride felt: "We have to put the brakes on and catch our breath." And so builders, contractors, and property owners may have to sit out the summer and early fall building season. And anyway, the mayor thought he might change the members of the committee that considers the variances. So if you are selling, buying, or making plans for property anywhere near wetlands…well, cool it and catch your breath, too.

One count of "electronic media advertising"

The East Hampton Town Code Enforcement Department went into action in the village of Montauk where a homeowner was charged with six counts of "excessive turnover" for renting his home to different groups on different weekends. Another homeowner was charged with one count of "excessive turnover" and one count of "electronic medium advertising" of his rentals on internet sites. Later, he was hit with other counts that carry $500 to $1000 fines per count and a possible six months in prison.

Both homeowners were renting out their own property, but renting it too often, to too many people—and even advertising this—is a matter for town "Code," which divines "the public interest" (but not the interests of the two homeowners or the renters) in matters of frequency of rental and all related matters. The decision to rent more or less frequently might be considered private in some towns; but they do not have the nationally recognized character of our town.

Relegated to page A11 was a story on the looming threat to our town of 'thin-ply plastic bags'—not a zoning matter, but an example of the same law-by-right-thinking. East Hampton is considering a ban on them, but the public interest, aesthetics, and character of thin-ply plastic bags apparently are not yet readily discernible. The town is seeking input from the "business sector" (not 'businessmen,' we deal in collectives, here), and the town's litter and energy sustainability committees.

There *already* is a ban on thin-ply plastic bags in East Hampton Village, where the requirements of character are clearer; under consideration now is extending it to the town as a whole. Town Supervisor Larry Cantwell seemed to reach a bit beyond town limits to put the bags threat in context: "When you look what's happening globally with plastic products in the environment…it's having a devastating impact."

Of course, there are literally millions of plastic products and just as many relevant "environments" "globally," and no assessment of the benefits of "plastic products" versus the alleged devastation they cause. And how it all relates to single-ply plastic bags in our town is a matter of judgment, to put it nicely. But if the East Hampton upholders of the town's public interest, taste, and global responsibility should decree it, any business using thin-ply plastic bags will be fined and its owners threatened with prison.

Did I mention that this year East Hampton spent millions to purchase 19 acres of farmland to prevent its development as housing for older residents? Again, not strictly zoning, but related. The town is now entertaining proposals for uses more in the public interest, taste, and character of our town? The latest hot proposal made page 1 of the *Star*. Henry C. "Chip" Blazer proposes to grow aronia berries, which he and his partner describe as a new "super food."

No decision has been made on how an aronia berry farm would complement our town's character; other proposals are being considered.

That is just one week (actually just the highlights of one week, as reported by the *Star*) in one town's struggle to assert and enforce correct thinking about the use of private property. If the same efforts were made to enforce correct thinking about speech, the press, or religious matters, within a year there would be no real right to freedom of speech, press, or worship.

Just as there is no real right to property; there is just an endless series of permissions.

What can we do about this virtual Sharia law for property—a local tyranny of taste, moral sensibility, aesthetic preferences, and merely fashionable opinion over the individual's property?

Make a "taking" a real taking

An amendment to the *U.S. Constitution* would give us one law, one standard, for all citizens in every state. It could be worded as are our other Constitutional guarantees: "Congress shall make no law abridging the right to the use and disposal of private property." Well, someday, perhaps—when we have overcome our religious-based dichotomy that holds that the individual's judgment when it comes to speech, press, and religion is sacred (because "spiritual"?) and cannot be subject to collective veto, but the individual's judgment when it comes to using his property is secondary (because "material"?). Secondary to the "public interest" (or "aesthetic" or "recognized character") as perceived and enforced by the collective.

But there is another way, also related to the *Constitution*, but not requiring a national consensus and still leaving localities room for maneuver. It is the Constitutional guarantee of "due process," especially as related to "takings."

At this time, government commits a "taking" only when it seizes private property by eminent domain, takes it from the owner to be put to supposedly essential public uses. The crucial question, here, is what constitutes a "taking." If East Hampton enacts a zoning or other law that prohibits me from developing my property because there are Piping Plovers nesting on it, it has not seized my property. But is has seized, in effect, much or most of its economic value. Is that not, in effect, a taking?'

The issue is not entirely theoretical. The Institute of Justice—a nonprofit, public-interest law firm in Washington, D.C.—has supported cases where a local zoning decree reduces the value of private property, arguing that it is, in effect, a "taking" of the property. This suffered a setback in 2002, when the Supreme Court avoided the "takings" question by means of a very narrow ruling. But the approach could be a remarkably fruitful and powerful direction for future litigation. Imagine if the East Hampton Town Zoning Board of Appeals—when it required Dylan's Candy Bar to power wash the sidewalk daily, install trash containers, and limit its sales to a specific area of the store—had to assess the total economic costs, and pay them from the public treasury. Or if a developer prevented from building because of proximity to wetlands had to be compensated for economic loss?

After all, every such decree to regulate and limit the use of private property is handed down in "the public interest." The "public" want wetlands? Let the public pay. The "public" want views that "please the eye"? Let them pay. I submit to you that if every zoning and other local limitation on property required the town to compensate owners for economic loss, the scope of the genuine "public" interest would shrink drastically. There would be room to maneuver, but that room would be subsidized not by depriving the individual of the value of his property, but by the "public" in whose interest the government supposedly acts.

This would be a giant stride in increasing the liberty of the individual, his right to act on his own judgment within his own domain. It would return to the marketplace—to contracts, covenants, rental agreements, consumer support or avoidance, boycotts, and all the other complex means of voluntary cooperation for mutual benefit—the decision about what uses of private property produce the greatest value as reckoned by the plebiscite of consumer choice. There are whole books about how this works.

In truth, there is no "public interest," only the interests of some individuals trumping the interests of others. As surely as Sharia law, much of zoning (perhaps not all) is the enforcement of one set of preferences. And

147

that is incompatible with a nation founded upon the rule of law, not the rule of men.

Published on *Financial Sense* on August 20, 2014.

The Unfair Distribution of Economic Freedom
January 2015)

When the World Economic Forum opened in Davos, Switzerland, Wednesday—bringing together 2,500 top corporate CEOs, 40 government leaders, NGO campaigners for many causes, and leading economists and political pundits—the statistic echoing off the Alps was: "The top 1% will have more wealth than the remaining 99% of the people" in the world by 2016. The source of that statistic is Oxfam, the British anti-poverty charity, which timed its report on world wealth equality for this year's Davos meeting.

Does it sound better to say that about 73 million individuals (1% of the 7.3 billion world population) control about half of the world's wealth? Or that to be in the top 1.0% you need $798,000 in total assets, including your home and retirement savings? Not really, although I just discovered that I am not a struggling retired guy, looking for a new job at 70, but one of the world's elite 1%.

Nor is it very reassuring to point out that our species, since the year 2000, has doubled its wealth from $117 trillion to $263 trillion in 2014. At least, we—some of us—still know how to make money! A great deal of that new wealth has been created in China, which, though the Communist one-party dictatorship retains a tight grip on politics, has opted for a market economy, freeing up hundreds of millions of Chinese to become richer. Much the same is true of India.

But that leaves us with about 20% of the world's population controlling 90% of its wealth, with the other 10% of wealth left to the remaining 80% of the world's population. So are some people are very good at building wealth, and lots of people are lousy at it?

The big decision-makers landing at Davos in their private jets (big traffic jams are expected at small airports) ought to take a look at another study—not quite as up-to-the-moment as Oxfam's, but more suggestive of solutions.

The 2014 "Index of Economic Freedom," the 20th in a series jointly published by *The Wall Street Journal* and the Heritage Foundation, rigorously rates the degree of economic freedom of 186 nations. The survey is probing, and the rankings merciless (for example, the United States no longer is rated "free" economically; that distinction goes to Hong Kong, Singapore, Australia, Switzerland, and Canada).

But what the Davos participants should ponder, even as they take the world's income inequality seriously, is what the "Index of Economic Freedom" calls the "correlates" of economic freedom:

"Economies rated 'free' or 'mostly free' in the 2014 *Index* enjoy average incomes that are more than three times higher than average incomes in all other countries and more than 10 times higher than the average incomes of 'repressed' economies. Economic freedom is key to enhancing overall well-being, taking into account other factors such as health, education, security, and political governance."

So perhaps there are not populations "good" at creating wealth: There are only populations free to create wealth. As the Davos decision-makers ponder wealth inequality, some may be tempted to reach for the usual levers of government: regulation and taxation to redistribute wealth. Certainly, given the themes of this year's meeting, they will be bombarded with arguments to increase climate pollution targets and energy regulations (Al Gore will take center stage).

They should weigh the cost of reducing economic freedom even as they tout the supposed benefits of environmental regulations, energy regulations, tax policy, banking regulations, and other buttons governments like to press.

When economic freedom, even in a political dictatorship like the People's Republic of China, brings wealth to hundreds of millions, it also brings to them access to education, health care, and security. And in the end, it brings aspiration to political freedom and the power to fight for it.

In an era when economic growth is driven as never before by innovation, when knowledge and invention are the great "natural resource," the freedom to create, invest, produce, and trade no longer is merely an "advantage"—it is the life or death of the wealth of nations. If the movers and shakers at Davos care about the opportunity for wealth of untold billions around the globe, they will talk about only one government policy: *laissez faire*.

That is the message that should be echoing from the Alps this week.

Rich and Free

The International Monetary Fund "World Economic Outlook Database" of April. 2013 (http://www.imf.org/external/pubs/ft/weo/2013/01/weodata /index.aspx), ranks countries according to their wealth per capita (Gross Domestic Product based on purchasing-power parity divided by population). Here are the 15 countries that top that list in order of their wealth. Next to each country, however, is a very different ranking (shown in parenthesis).

It comes from the *2014 Index of Economic Freedom* prepared annually by the *Wall Street Journal* and Heritage Foundation and now in its 20th year. The index ranks countries according to their degree of economic freedom based on such factors as respect for property rights, degree of economic regulation, and labor freedom. The number in parenthesis is that country's economic freedom, with #1 the most free.

> Qatar (#30)
> Luxembourg (#16)
> Singapore (#2)
> Norway (#32)
> Brunei (#40)
> Hong Kong (#1)
> United States (#12)
> United Arab Emirates (#28)
> Switzerland (#4)
> Australia (#3)
> Canada (#6)
> Austria (#24)
> Ireland (#9)
> Netherlands (#15)
> Sweden (#20)

The list will surprise most readers and in some evoke skepticism—such lists always do. Both national wealth and economic freedom are complex, in practice if not in theory, and I don't intend to try to explain (rationalize?) every ranking on the list.

The oil-rich nations with exceedingly small populations (Qatar, Brunei, United Arab Emirates, and Norway) are distinct outliers. They are the only nations among the 15 wealthiest nations with economic freedom rankings above 25—and as high (low in economic freedom) as 40 in the case of Brunei. Their only product is oil. They did not create it, nor did they figure out how to drill for it and ship it: Western companies did that. Economic freedom is not the dominant factor in their wealth. Nevertheless, the *Index* creates categories, and, for example, in the elite category "free" there are only six nations. But in the next category, "mostly free," there are 28. Three out of the four oil-producing nations in the top 15 in wealth make it into that "mostly free" category.

Another thing to notice is that five of the nations in the elite "free" category are also in the top 15 in wealth. The exception is New Zealand, rated "free" but not among the 15 most wealthy. I said I would not try to "rationalize" the list; but I will mention that after 10 years of labor-dominated government, New Zealand voters brought back the center-right National Party, led by Prime Minister John Keys with an explicit commitment to economic liberalization. Economic freedom is relatively new to New Zealand.

Well, what about Sweden, ranking 15th in wealth but 20th in economic freedom? Again, Sweden is ranked "mostly free" in its economy. Sweden also is famous for its 'socialism,' but that takes the form of an extensive welfare state. Certainly, taxation and borrowing to support a welfare state weaken an economy, but the "production" side of Sweden is left relatively free. One other factor also is relevant: up until 1950, when Sweden began its experiment with the welfare state (not really "socialism"), it was for a century among the most economically liberal and fastest growing nations in Europe. You do not squander that heritage overnight.

To me, the mystery on the list is Austria, ranked #12 in wealth per capita but ranked #24 in economic freedom. Again, Austria's economy is ranked "mostly free," and it has a small, very homogeneous population, and a long tradition of higher education. It also leaves most economic decisions to negotiations between workers and employers (for example, Austria has no minimum wage), with government an umpire.

Finally, what about the great United States, a world economic engine, home of the *laissez faire* capitalist tradition. In 2014, the *Index* ranked it only "mostly free," along with a sundry 28 other "mostly free" nations. Why? This must be the most disturbing anomaly on the list and I will let the *Index* describe it:

"Since [2006]…, it has suffered a dramatic decline of almost 6 points, with particularly large losses in property rights, freedom from corruption, and control of government spending. The U.S. is the only country to have recorded a loss of economic freedom each of the past seven years. The overall U.S. score decline from 1995 to 2014 is 1.2 points, the fourth worst drop among advanced economies." (http://www.heritage.org/index/ranking)

Sic transit gloria mundi.

Published on "Savvy Street," January 23, 2015.

Recommended Reading

In writing every essay in this book, and choosing what to write about, my viewpoint has been that of a classical liberal, the tradition of Adam Smith, David Ricardo, and, jumping to our time, Ludwig von Mises of the Austrian school of economics, the Nobel laureate in economics, Milton Friedman, and such legendary economic journalists as Henry Hazlitt, whose classic *Economics in One Lesson* never will be out of date. Any of these authors will deepen and elaborate the ideas suggested here.

But I arrive at my view of economics and political economy standing on the shoulders of a philosophy that is called "Objectivism." That is the name the famous, widely revered American novelist and thinker, Ayn Rand, gave to her philosophy. She is best known for her epic novel *Atlas Shrugged* and the literary classic *The Fountainhead*, but she made explicit the political philosophy and economic system implied by the unrepeatably inspiring stories told in those novel in *Capitalism: The Unknown Ideal*. If you read *Atlas Shrugged*, you will require no further guidance from me. And *Capitalism: The Unknown Ideal* may be the greatest single integration of formal philosophy, political philosophy, and cultural analysis available in print.

The financial panic of 2008 and the ensuing stock-market crash and Great Recession has helped at least one industry: the production of books to explain how it all happened. If the reasoning in this book appeals to you, then start with *The Financial Crisis and the Free Market Cure: Why Pure Capitalism is the World Economy's Only Hope*, by John Allison (McGraw-Hill, 2012). Allison's book presents events from the same point of view as this book, but, of course, at 320 pages, is far more detailed and comprehensive. Also, Mr. Allison was a foremost bank CEO throughout the crisis and describes event after event from the point of view of a deeply involved player.

If you wish to explore the arguments in *Not Half Free* that take human liberty and its paramount value as their starting point, then read not only the works of Ayn Rand and the classic liberals, but a modern statement of the libertarian philosophy: *Libertarianism: A Primer*, by David Boaz (Free Press, 1998). Executive director of the foremost libertarian think-tank, the Cato Institute, Boaz articulates the power and benevolence of human liberty in every area of human life.

If you start with these books, you will discover—if you are inspired to continue—the intellectually thrilling literature of freedom: the freedom that begins with each person's choice to think, to use reason to engage the world, and can be translated into the principles of a society that protects the individual's precious freedom to act on his own judgment, and, finally, the unprecedented betterment of every nation that has made protection of freedom the priority of government.

You may keep abreast of critiques of the kind found in *Not Half Free* on several Web sites: www.atlassociety.com, www.financialsense.com, www.savvystreet.com, and www.cato.org.

These will lead you to many additional thinkers, books, and Web pages devoted to making the case that laissez-faire capitalism is not only the most productive economic system, but the only political economy based upon consistent recognition of the rights of man.

Books by Walter Donway

Poetry

Touched by Its Rays

How Glad I Am for Man, Tonight

Novels,

The Lailly Worm:
A Young Lawyer, a Dungeon in East Hampton,

And One Chance to Fight Back

O Human Child

The Price of Hannah Blake: Victorian England's
Secret Sex Scandal

The Way the Wind Blew:
They Battled America's First Terrorists

Nonfiction Works

"You're Probably from Holden, If…": Growing
Up in a Vanishing New England

Not Half Free: The Myth that America is Capitalist

"You're Probably from Worcester, If..."

History's Luckiest Puppy: The Story of Rin-tin-tin

Short Stories and Personal Essays

Holidays Frightened My Father and Other Stories and Personal Narratives

Nothing but a Gun (novella)

Remember To Scream (novella)

Walter Donway

With weekly commentary in online publications, Walter Donway has become one of today's most original and powerful voices advocating a philosophically grounded libertarianism.

Since the 1970's, when he became a widely published analyst and critic of the drive to create a "national health care system," he has been writing about politics, political economy, and the long-term curtailment of individual freedom by the metastasizing of the interventionist-welfare state. Writing from the perspective of Objectivism, the philosophy of Ayn Rand, he has attacked the destruction of capitalism--by which he always means *laissez faire* capitalism--in commentary that has appeared in *Private Practice, Medical World News*, the *Wall Street Journal, Newsday, Pharos*, the *New Individualist*, the *Occasional Review, Commonweal, Pharos*, and other publications, as well as on Web sites such as the *Atlas Society, Financial Sense*, the *Atlasphere*, and *Savvy Street*.

Beginning his career as business and finance reporter for the Worcester *Telegram*, he has been a foundation executive, fundraising consultant, and freelance journalist in New York City since 1974. He was a founding trustee of the Atlas Society, served on its board for two decades, and edited its first publication, *The IOS Journal*.

Ten years ago, he turned full-time to writing and has published four novels, including *The Way the Wind Blew*, a thriller about New Left violence in the 1970's; and two books about small-town rural life in New England just after WWII, including *"You're Probably from Holden If…": Growing Up in A Vanishing New England*. All are published by Romantic Revolution Books, a publishing imprint that he created and manages.

He lives with his wife, Robin, in New York City and East Hampton.